The Sacrificial System
of the
Old Testament

Walter C. Wright
Member American Institute of Accountants

UNION GOSPEL PRESS
CLEVELAND, OHIO

CONTENTS

FOREWORD

It is in line with the title of this book that its scope is confined to the sacrificial ritual instituted by Moses in Egypt and in the wilderness, except for some discussion in the appendices of ordinances of a later time. It is true that sacrifices were offered from the earliest times with Divine approval, but there is no instance prior to the days of Moses of sacrifices being **enjoined** upon the people of God as a system of worship and a means of approach. This is not to say that no such system had ever been inaugurated: the implications are that it had. But if this were the case there must have been a providential reason for the silence of the Scriptures concerning it. The approval of the offering of Abel; the spontaneous burnt sacrifices of Noah; the demand made upon Abraham's faith centuries afterwards, and the presentation of burnt offerings and peace offerings, at the time of the giving of the Law, suggest that the idea had been implanted in the mind of man by God, and the subsequent history of redemption gives the fullest support to this conclusion. From the very beginning God had in mind the sacrifice of His Son.

W. C. W.

CHAPTER 1

THE TABERNACLE OF TESTIMONY

THE congregation of Israel, consisting of hundreds of thousands of men, women and children encamped in the wilderness of Sinai around a central point on which was pitched an oblong tent, surrounded by a court which was encompassed by a screen of curtains of fine linen. This tent was their religious rallying point. Its design and proportions, and the materials with which it was constructed, as well as its furniture, had all been the subject of communications made to Moses on the Mount. It had been made after the pattern showed to him there.

No adequate consideration could be given to the sacrificial system of the Old Testament apart from this tabernacle, at the door of which the sacrifices were offered and about which the system centered itself. As a symbol, the tabernacle was a revelation of the way in which man might approach God. But the tabernacle was only one of a group of symbols any one of which was insufficient alone. The tabernacle could not be approached without the sacrificial offering, and the sacrificial offering could not be presented but by the priest. The tabernacle, priesthood and offerings were a group of symbols, constituting together the means of approach.

And so God says to Moses: "Let them make Me a sanctuary; that I may dwell among them" *(Exod. 25: 8)*.

There is in the human heart an urgent desire for some manifestation of the Deity on which the physical senses may fasten themselves. God made the human heart and He knows this. He was about to meet the hunger which this desire creates. He had called Moses up into the Mount, not only to give him the Law which could be heard with the ear, but the directions for erecting a tabernacle which could be seen with the eye. And in the impetuous treachery of their hearts, because Moses was absent for a month, the people melted their golden ornaments, the spoil which they had taken from the Egyptians, into the form of a calf, and worshipped it.

We could hardly credit the perfidy of the human heart were it not that there beat in our own breasts the fitful pulsations of that same treachery.

Think of what they had experienced during the last few months.

They had been delivered from a condition of intolerable bondage by the most signal interpositions of Divine power. They had seen every household in Egypt in mourning while they themselves had gone out without hurt. The armies of Pharaoh had pursued them, but those armies had perished in the waters of the Red Sea. In the early days of their wilderness experience they had been threatened with hunger, and bread had come down to them from Heaven to satisfy their need. They had been threatened with thirst, and water had come gushing out from a rock for them to drink. And, finally, they had come to Mount Sinai, and there they had heard the voice of the Living God speaking out of the earthquake and the fire.

And in the face of all this they renounce their allegiance.

If we carefully study the portions of the Book of Exodus which narrate the events which occurred while the multitude was encamped at Mount Sinai, we find that Moses ascended and descended the Mount seven times in receiving the directions which God gave him, and in exercising the office of Mediator for the people.

It was at the time of the fifth ascent that God gave him the directions for the construction of the tabernacle, and it was on that same occasion that he received the Tables of the Law, written with the finger of God.

This is how a part of the narrative reads:

"And Jehovah spake unto Moses, saying, Speak unto the Children of Israel, that they take for Me an offering: of every man whose heart maketh him willing ye shall take My offering. And this is the offering which ye shall take of them: gold, and silver, and brass, and blue, and purple, and scarlet, and fine linen, and goats' hair, and rams' skins dyed red, and sealskins, and acacia wood, oil for the light, spices for the anointing oil, and for the sweet incense, onyx stones, and stones to be set, for the ephod, and for the breastplate. And let them make Me a sanctuary; that I may dwell among them" (A. S. V.).

And that sanctuary was a tent.

But why was the dwelling in the form of a tent? Why was it not in the form of a palace or a cathedral? Was it not in the first place because the Children of Israel themselves were dwelling in tents? And in coming to dwell among them God took up His abode as one of them, to dwell as they were dwelling. That was not the only reason, as we shall see, but it is perhaps the most obvious and the most easily appreciated one.

There was a second reason why God chose a tent as His dwelling place. The tabernacle was to be a symbol of spiritualities and a type of His tenting among men in human form. This is undoubtedly what John refers to when he says: "And the Word became flesh, and tabernacled among us" *(John 1:14, marg. A. S. V.).*

But it was not just an ordinary tent. It was a tent, but there was no tent in the Camp of Israel which was at all like that tent. It was made according to the pattern showed in the Mount.

It is not the intention of this book to expound in detail the symbolism of the tent and its furnishings: that would require a volume. We suggest, however, in a general way that in the tabernacle, the offerings and the priests we have a **group** of related symbols and types; in the tabernacle and its furnishings we have a **composite** type, and in the tent itself we have a **pure** type.

Taking these three statements in their reverse order, we notice in the first place that the tent was a pure type, a type of Christ. Was it not first of all a type of Christ in its origin? How did the tabernacle originate? Was it an earthly thing or a heavenly thing? It was neither the one nor the other for it was both the one and the other. God contributed the pattern; the people contributed the materials. "Speak unto the Children of Israel, that they bring Me an heave offering" *(Exod. 25:2, marg.).* That is the one statement. "According to all that I shew thee, after the pattern of the tabernacle, and the pattern of all the instruments thereof, even so shall ye make it" *(Exod. 25:9).* That is the other statement.

Was not this the like of what occurred in the incarnation of Christ? Was Jesus Christ an earthly being or a Heavenly being? He was neither the one nor the other, for He was both the one and the other. **The Word became flesh.** Humanity contributed His nature; God contributed His personality.

But what about the **appearance** of the tabernacle?

How did it look from the outside? What was its aspect? What impression did the worshipper receive as he approached? The outermost covering was of badgers' skins. Do you remember what the prophet Isaiah said of the Servant of Jehovah? "He hath no form nor comeliness; and when we shall see Him, there is no beauty that we should desire Him". Christ was just as different from every other man as the tabernacle was from every other tent, but the singular charm of His personality, that which drew the throngs about Him, was not His outward aspect, not His appearance; it was something **within**. And what was the tabernacle like within? Gold and blue and purple and scarlet and fine twined linen. So was it with Christ. To those who looked at Him only from the outside He did not measure up to their expectations as a Messiah. He was a carpenter's son; He was not a graduate of the Rabbinical schools. "How knoweth this Man letters", they said, "having never learned"? But to those who had eyes to see within, how different their estimate! They could say with John: "we beheld His glory, the glory as of the Only Begotten of the Father, full of grace and truth". They had been inside the tent!

Yes, and there was something, you remember in the **construction** of the tent that spoke of His incarnation. And we are not left to speculation as to this. "The veil", the Writer of the Epistle to the Hebrews says, was "His flesh" (*Heb. 10:20*). The veil divided the Holy Place from the Most Holy Place. That curtain shut out the priests from the innermost shrine. Just so the life which Christ lived upon the earth stands, as it were, in between man and God. It erected an impossible standard; it was the "true life." The life of Jesus is beautiful to look at, to contemplate, but in itself it can only lead us to despair. It is only through the broken body that we can reach God. The veil symbolized that fact. And when Christ expired upon the cross, the veil of the temple was rent in twain from the top to the bottom.

In the tent itself, then, we have a pure type, a type of Christ. In the tabernacle and its furnishings, however, we appear to have a **composite** type. It might not be correct to say that the altar of incense, the table of shewbread, the lamp stand or the ark of the covenant were types of Christ, but together they appear to constitute a composite type of Messiah and Israel. Let us illustrate this. The shewbread was the "bread of the presence," or the "bread of the face." It was continually in the presence of, or before the face of, Jehovah. It was, therefore, in symbol, something which would continually satisfy God. There was, moreover, frankincense upon it, so that it was termed an offering of Jehovah "made by fire". It was also of fine flour, as the Meal Offering was. But there were twelve loaves; one for each of the tribes. These loaves were renewed every Sabbath.

As the Nation presented, week by week, these loaves with the frankincense, they were typically offering to God that which would perfectly satisfy Him, and only Christ can do that. But did not God see in the sabbatical offering of the twelve loaves an earnest of the presentation of renewed and restored Israel, in her consecrated completeness, in the millennial sabbath?

We might develop a similar line of thought in connection with the other furnishings of the tent, and find in them composite types. It is so with the lamp stand. The lights were renewed by the priests every evening, and burned through the night. When the tents of the people were in darkness the lights burned in the sacred tent. Jesus was indeed the Light of the

World, but does not Isaiah say to Israel: "Arise, shine; for thy light is come"? And then he adds: "For, behold, darkness shall cover the earth, and gross darkness the peoples; but Jehovah will rise upon thee, and His glory shall be seen upon thee" (A. S. V.).

And no less is this the case with the altar of incense and the ark. As we contemplate their spiritual significance we see in symbol those fundamental realities which Israel was called into being to express, but which can only be manifested through her to the world as she herself is organically connected with Christ.

And so, if we take the tent and its furnishings: the table of shewbread, the lamp stand, the altar of incense and the ark of the covenant, together with the tabernacle and all the spiritualities for which they stood, and **merge them together**, we have, as it were, a composite type of Messiah and Israel.

But not only do we have in the tent itself a pure type of Christ, and in the tabernacle and its furnishings a composite type of Messiah and Israel, we have also in the tabernacle, the offerings and the priesthood a group of related symbols and types.

This may become increasingly evident as we study the sacrificial ritual.

CHAPTER II.

THE ARK AND THE MERCY SEAT

IT was stated at the beginning of the first chapter that no adequate consideration could be given to the sacrificial system of the Old Testament apart from the tabernacle. But everything in the tabernacle was subordinate to the ark. Indeed, we might say that the tabernacle was a tent for the ark.

How was the ark made? It was a box, or chest, constructed of wood, probably acacia wood, and overlaid within and without with gold. The lid was made of pure gold, and was laid upon the top. It was kept in place by a crown, or molding, and at the two ends of the lid, and of one piece with it, worked out of solid gold, were two cherubimic figures, the one at the one end and the other at the other.

Of what was the ark a symbol? It was a symbol of the Divine government, of the throne of God. If you will turn to the third chapter of Jeremiah you will find this suggested in the form of a contrast.

> "In those days, saith Jehovah, they shall say no more, The ark of the covenant of Jehovah * *. At that time they shall call Jerusalem the throne of Jehovah" *(Jer. 3:16, 17).*‡

And in the ark, the symbol of the throne of God, was deposited the Law. It was a perfect law but it was a violated law. What does God do with a violated law? The ark suggests three answers to that question.

I. He **maintains** it. You recall that as Moses descended from the Mount with the tables of the Law in his hand, and witnessed the idolatry of the people, he threw down the tables and broke them upon the

‡See also Jer. 17:12; Ezek. 10:1.

mountain *(Exod. 32:19)*. But God called Moses up
into the mountain again, and wrote the Law upon new
tables *(Deut. 10:4)*. And then Moses deposited them
in the ark. Now you cannot understand the significance of that action unless you recognize the symbolism of the ark. If the ark was merely a box for safe
keeping of what might be deposited within it, there
was no particular meaning in depositing the Law
therein. It might indicate that it was a precious thing,
but that is all. But the depositing of the tables of the
law in the ark indicated that God intended to maintain a violated law, for the ark was a symbol of the
Divine government.

There must be moral and spiritual principles of a
very fundamental character embodied in the Decalogue. Its place at the heart of the Mosaic legislation
implies as much; the fact that God wrote it with His
own finger confirms the impression. How searchingly
spiritual the Decalogue is! At its two **extremities** we
have the ideal relation of man towards God and of
man towards man. A **perfect** heart toward God; a
perfect heart toward man: these are the requirements.
And these deeply spiritual demands **fence in** the ten
commandments.

On a certain occasion the question was put to Jesus:
"which is the great commandment in the law"? And
then He did a remarkable thing. He took a fragment
of a sentence in the Book of Deuteronomy and a fragment of another sentence in the Book of Leviticus,
and He put them together and said that on those two
commandments hung all the Law and the Prophets.
But the most remarkable thing about that declaration
was this: That the first of those statements was a paraphrase of the first commandment in the Decalogue,
and the second statement was a paraphrase of the last
commandment in the Decalogue.

"No other gods before Me". That is the first commandment in the Decalogue. "Thou shalt love the Lord thy God with all thy heart, and with all thy soul, and with all thy mind"; that, He says, is the "first and great commandment". But the last commandment is this: "thou shalt not covet". "Thou shalt love thy neighbour as thyself". That, He says, is the second commandment. The two together comprehend all (Matt. 22:36-40; Deut. 6:5; Lev. 19:18).

Let us look at these tables of the Law a little more particularly. The first group of these laws seeks to regulate man's relation to God. The last group seeks to regulate man's relation to man. The true division of these **ten words** would seem to be, not into two groups of five and five but rather an arrangement of three, one, and six. When we group the ten commandments in this way we have two groups united together or held apart, as the case may be, by an injunction which is in a class by itself, being a ceremonial, and not a moral, law. Thus, in the very heart of the Decalogue there is an expression of the impotence of the Law as a justifying agency, for the meaning of Sabbath is: "cease to do". It is in agreement with this that there is such reiterated admonishment in connection with the Feasts of Jehovah, and particularly the Day of Atonement, to do "no work"; "no servile work"; "no manner of work".

With such an arrangement we'have at the head of the manward table the command to recognize and honor those who are God's representatives, and who, in the period of tutelage stand in the place of God. Following that we have a fourfold desecration of human rights:

"Thou shalt not kill". Thou shalt not rob a man of his life.

"Thou shalt not commit adultery". Thou shalt not rob a man of his marital rights.

"Thou shalt not steal". Thou shalt not rob a man of his property.

"Thou shalt not bear false witness". Thou shalt not rob a man of his reputation. And finally, that which goes to the heart of the matter; thou shalt not **want to**: thou shalt not **desire** anything that is thy neighbour's.

This fundamental law, this law of perfection, God determines to maintain. He writes it with His own finger on stone, and He requires it to be placed in the ark, which is the symbol of the Divine government.

II. In the second place, He not only maintains it, He **mediates** it. And this again is illustrated in the ark.

We have already noticed how the ark was made, with a lid kept in place by a molding. This lid was called the propitiatory, or as the Revised Version renders it, the "mercy seat". It is the same word as that used in the Epistle to the Romans where Christ is spoken of as a "propitiation" through faith in His Blood *(See also I John 2:2 and 4:10)*. This lid was an integral part of the ark, and the ark was a symbol of the throne of God, and in the ark were the tables of the violated law. And once a year, on the Day of Atonement, the lid was sprinkled with blood. The blood was sprinkled also **before** the mercy seat. This is God's way of dealing with sin, and of satisfying the demands of righteousness. The blood symbolizes a life forfeited, or a life laid down—a surrendered life. But it is not the blood of the transgressor that is thus brought into the presence of God. The blood upon the mercy seat is the symbol of God's own life; no other life would meet the demands of perfect holiness. It is **His** life which is laid down. Thus He mediates a violated law; He comes between the law and the transgressor with the virtue of His own obedience; He was "obedient unto death". "By His stripes we are healed."

But although the blood is the symbol of the very life of God, yet it is presented by Another, and that is symbolized by the sprinkling **before** the ark. But the blood was not only sprinkled **upon** the mercy seat, and **before** the mercy seat, it was also put upon the horns of the altar of incense, and this symbolized the fact that it was presented prevailingly, for the horns were the symbols of power *(Lev. 4:6, 7)*.

But God not only maintains and mediates a violated law:

III. He **magnifies** it. "And over it the cherubims of glory shadowing the mercy seat". There is a good deal of mystery surrounding these creatures. Representations of them formed an integral part of the lid of the ark. They were all of one piece with the mercy seat, worked out of a solid piece of gold. The description reads thus:

"And thou shalt make two cherubims of gold, of beaten work shalt thou make them, in the two ends of the mercy seat. And make one cherub on the one end, and the other cherub on the other end: even of the mercy seat shall ye make the cherubims on the two ends thereof. And the cherubims shall stretch forth their wings on high, covering the mercy seat with their wings, and their faces shall look one to another; toward the mercy seat shall the faces of the cherubims be" *(Exod. 25:18-20)*.

We meet with the cherubims several times in the Scriptures. The description, when it is given, varies and does not seem to be self-consistent *(Gen. 3:24; Ezek. 1:4-10; 10:14, 20; Rev. 4:6-8)*.

They appear to be symbols, but they would seem to be more than symbols—to be an order of Heavenly beings. However, on the mercy seat they are symbols and nothing more. What are they symbols of? Are

they not symbols of creature intelligence, representing
creaturehood in its highest forms? The lion is the
king of the untamed beasts: the ox in that day was
chief of domesticated animals; the eagle is the monarch
of the air; man is the crown of creaturehood.

But they not only represent creaturehood in its
highest forms, they symbolize creation, as thus represented, manifesting moral dispositions. Will you
notice their attitudes. Their wings are outstretched
over the mercy seat, and their faces are downward
bent. They gaze upon the symbols of the Divine government in adoring wonder. They seem to represent
vigilant jealousy for the Divine glory; brooding over
the ark, gazing upon it with a wistful and reverent
wonder, and a consuming jealousy for the glory of
God.

But if the ark is a symbol of the throne, then we
have the conception of a throne in a temple; of government exercised in the atmosphere of the sanctuary,
and in the presence of those mediating ministries for
which the tabernacle and the temple stood. This is
one of the most marvelous conceptions which the
human mind can contemplate, and it pervades the
Scriptures.

"Jerusalem", Jeremiah says, shall be called the
"throne of Jehovah" (A. S. V.). Isaiah tells us that in
the last days the word of Jehovah shall go forth from
Jerusalem (Is. 2:3). And at the end of that section,
at the close of the fourth chapter, he says that upon
every dwelling place of Mount Zion, and upon her
assemblies, there shall be a cloud and smoke by day,
and the shining of a flaming fire by night. There must
be an allusion here to the Shekinah glory. Just as that
glory covered the ark, even so over Jerusalem there

will be a canopy of glory. **Jerusalem** shall be the throne of Jehovah.

A throne in a temple. Before the ark, and intimately connected with it, was the altar of incense. A prayer room before a throne!

A throne in a temple. Turn to Ezekiel 43:7. The prophet seems to be seeing in a vision the idealized temple. He is taken up by the Spirit into the inner court (*vs. 5*), and the glory of Jehovah filled the house. And a voice speaks out of the house: "Son of Man, the place of My throne".

A throne in a temple. That is the conception which is before us in the vision which Isaiah has as a young man. He sees Jehovah upon a **throne**, high and lifted up, and His skirts fill the **temple** *(Is. 6:1)*.

A throne in a temple. We come to the last book of Scripture and there again we find the same conception. In the seventh chapter we read of those who came out of the great tribulation, that they are **before** the **throne**, and serve day and night in His **temple**. And again in the seventeenth verse of the sixteenth chapter, when the seventh angel pours out his vial into the air, there comes a great voice **out of the temple of Heaven**, from the **throne**.

We may see more fully the meaning of this connection of the throne and the temple as these studies proceed.

CHAPTER III.

THE PRIESTS OF ISRAEL

WE do not know how or when the idea of priesthood came to be communicated to man, but on the one hand it would seem to inhere in the very nature of God, and on the other hand it meets the imperative needs of sinful men.

The first mention of priesthood is in the fourteenth chapter of Genesis, where Melchisedec is introduced. He is spoken of as priest of the Most High God. The Writer of the Epistle to the Hebrews says that he was priest of Salem: this name may be an abbreviation for Jerusalem. The fact of his priesthood at some center in Palestine, and the esteem in which he was held by Abraham, suggest much unrecorded religious history. It may be that the Melchisedec priesthood was the expression of a revelation which God had made to the earlier inhabitants of the Promised Land, and that the moral conditions which called for their extermination were the consequence of an apostasy from the true religion. The impression which is made upon us by the record of Melchisedec is one of spiritual solitariness.

At a later date, three generations subsequent, there is mention of a pagan priesthood in Egypt. And Joseph married the daughter of an Egyptian priest. Moses also married the daughter of a priest.

When God entered into covenant with the Children of Israel at Mount Sinai the idea of priesthood was assumed to be a familiar one, and it was with a view to priesthood that they were separated from the other nations of the earth. They were to be a "kingdom of priests, and an holy nation". Originally, the firstborn of the entire nation had been set apart for God, but the Levites were substituted for the firstborn. Of the tribe of Levi, a family was taken to minister at the altar, the family of Aaron, and of that family one man was chosen to come before God in the Most Holy Place. That is how the Aaronic priesthood came into being.

The functions of the Levites and of the priests were not limited, however, to the worship of the tabernacle and attendance upon the altar. They were to be teachers of the Law and advisors of the Judges (*Deut. 17:8-11; Mal. 2:7; Ezek. 44:24*).

In the fifth chapter of the Epistle to the Hebrews, the Writer tells us what are the qualifications of a true priest. He must be a man; he must be compassionate; he must have approached the altar for himself. And as such, he must have been "called of God".

The priest personified in his office and ministry the spiritual situation which had resulted in a distance between man and God. This is emphasized at every turn. Even the Levites could not approach officially to the altar, although they ministered at the tabernacle. The worshipper could come into the outer court; that was all. The priests might enter into the Holy Place but they might not go into the Holy of Holies. And even the high priest might go there but once a year.

But whilst the priest, as it were, kept the worshipper at a distance from God, he expressed the possibility of approach, for he himself drew near. And he drew near on behalf of the worshipper.

And his ministry indicated the way of approach. It was the way of a life laid down—surrendered up.

We have already noticed that the Aaronic priests are expressly said to have been called of God. For what were they called? What was the ministry of the priests designed to accomplish? Every spiritually minded student of Scripture recognizes the fact that the ministry of the priesthood symbolized spiritualities, and that the priests themselves were types of Christ. In those aspects of their ministry they may have accomplished more for us than for the men of their own day: we are privileged to see in their actions what their contemporaries could not discern. But their ministry was not merely symbolic, and it was not exclusively for us. It had meanings as well as limitations for the people of that day. We desire, therefore, to make a threefold enquiry as to the Aaronic ministry in relation to the men of that day, and to ask:

1. What the priests of Israel did for the men of their own day.

2. What they could not do.

3. What their actions and their impotence symbolized.

First then, what did the Aaronic priests accomplish for their contemporaries? Three things suggest themselves.

(a) They represented the Nation before God. The Nation, as such, was in covenant relationship with God. This was a unique situation in the history of the Race. God has from time to time made covenants with individual men. He did so with Noah, with Abraham, with David. But He did not make a covenant with Moses. The covenant at Sinai was a national one. The state churches of our own day attempt to approximate the situation which existed between God and Israel, but they do so only in name. The essential difference is that God does not sanction them. The nation is **not** a church. But in Israel the congregation **was** the church. The covenant was national. And that is a Divine ideal. It is embedded in the very structure of the tabernacle. The ark is behind the altar of incense; the throne is in the temple. And in the ideal state there is to be a priest upon the throne.

And the nation and the church being one, it followed that religious rites and civil ordinances could sometimes hardly be distinguished the one from the other—the dividing line was obscure; perhaps sometimes there was no dividing line at all.

And so the **approach** of the people was largely of an external character. And even the operations of the Spirit of God were physical in their character. And thus the **regulations** in connection with the approach often concerned matters which were of indifference as to morality. They were ceremonial. (And yet there often was a close connection between the ceremonial requirement and the moral life.)

But although it was an external approach, it was an external approach to a **holy God**. And it was by way of an altar and with blood, for, nationally as well as individually, the people were under sentence of death.

This outward ritual, therefore, suggested something deeper than itself, and that brings us to the second thing that the priests of Israel did for the men of their own day.

(b) They kept before the people the reality of the Unseen. There was a holy mystery about the ministry of the priests which must have excited the sacred curiosity of the people. As they saw the priests passing into the Holy Place, day by day, must they not have wondered what might transpire in that antechamber of the Divine presence? But much more on the Day of days, once a year, when the high priest went within the veil.

The very recollection of the **fact** of the Unseen is a spiritual stimulant. The very presence of the tabernacle amongst them was a reminder that there was a fellowship to be aspired to, and a God to know.

And then, they not only represented the Nation before God, and kept before the people the reality of the Unseen,

(c) They mediated a Divine disposition.

We are told in the Epistle to the Hebrews that it is one of the qualifications of a true priest that he have "compassion on the ignorant, and on them that are out of the way" (5:2). That was, of course, the **ideal**: it was often unrealized. But ideally the priests were to express the disposition of God to sinful men. And it was only as expressing such a disposition that they could suitably approach God on behalf of the people. That approach was of an external character. Nevertheless, because the people were men who had been made in the image of God, and had **consciences**, even the outward ritual encouraged in them expectations which were in keeping with the spiritual realities which the ritual symbolized.

These, then, were some of the things which the priests of Israel did for the men of their own day.

But, in the second place, notice: What they could not do.

(a) The ritual provided no means of expiation for high handed sins. It may be it is this that the Apostle has in mind in Acts 13:38, 39 where he alludes to things "from which ye could not be justified by the Law of Moses". Whether such sins were intended to be covered by the sacrifices of the Day of Atonement is not perhaps clear, but a man could not commit murder, and bring an offering as an expiation, and so

end the matter. The civil statute was binding that
the murderer must be slain.

(b) Nor could the priestly ministrations at Israel's
altars make the conscience "perfect". They could not
acquit. There was always a sense of incompleteness,
of insufficiency. Else, says the Writer of the Epistle
to the Hebrews, why were the sacrifices repeated
every year? More or less dimly or clearly, according
to the spiritual apprehension of the worshipper, they
spoke of something for which penitence longed, but
which no external ritual could communicate.

(c) And the priests could not bring the people into
the very presence of God. There was always something between them and God. There was a distance.

But notice further, and in the third place: What the
actions and the impotence of the priesthood symbolized to the people. Observe three things:

(a) That God wanted them to draw near; else why
should He have appointed the ritual?

(b) That they could not come into His immediate
presence, else why were they represented by one
man who went to and fro on their behalf?

(c) That every approach must satisfy the requirements of holiness.

They kept a continual table before Jehovah; they
were constantly presenting that which satisfied His
heart. There was a perpetual oblation of Christ. And
the blood was poured at the foot of the altar and put
upon its horns. It was therefore the **foundation** of
their acceptance, and the **means** by which they were
to **prevail**.

And that same blood was taken to the altar of incense. And it was taken to the mercy seat, to the

throne of God. There was a direct line between the altar and the ark, between the place of sacrifice and the throne.

The **actions** of the priests in connection with the ritual will be spoken of in a subsequent chapter.

CHAPTER IV.

SACRIFICES AND OFFERINGS

Hebrews 5:1; 8:3; 9:9

THE following passages of Scripture form a background to the subject considered in this chapter:

"Every high priest taken from among men is ordained for men in things pertaining to God, that he may offer both gifts and sacrifices for sins" *(Heb. 5:1)*.

"Wherewith shall I come before Jehovah, and bow myself before the high God? shall I come before Him with burnt-offerings, with calves a year old? will Jehovah be pleased with thousands of rams, or with ten thousands of rivers of oil? shall I give my first-born for my transgression, the fruit of my body for the sin of my soul? He hath shewed thee, O man, what is good; and what doth Jehovah require of thee, but to do justly, and to love kindness, and to walk humbly with thy God"? *(Mic. 6:6-8, A. S. V.)*.

"Thus saith Jehovah of hosts, the God of Israel: Add your burnt-offerings unto your sacrifices, and eat ye flesh. For I spake not unto your fathers, nor commanded them in the day that I brought them out of the land of Egypt, concerning burnt-offerings or sacrifices: but this thing I commanded them, saying, Hearken unto My voice, and I will be your God, and ye shall be My people; and walk ye in all the ways that I command you, that it may be well with you" *(Jer. 7:21-23)*.

"But go ye and learn what that meaneth, I will have mercy and not sacrifice" *(Matt. 9:13)*.

"Wherefore when He cometh into the world, He saith, Sacrifice and offering Thou wouldest not, but a body hast thou prepared Me: in burnt offerings and sacrifices for sin thou hast had no pleasure. Then said I, Lo, I come (in the volume of the Book it is written of Me,) to do Thy will, O God" *(Heb. 10:5-7)*.

There are certainly apparent contradictions in some of those statements, when we regard them as constituting parts of a self-consistent revelation. Shall we therefore endeavor to find the basis of agreement between them by enquiring earnestly into the spiritual inwardness of the sacrificial system.

From the very earliest days of human history men have brought sacrifices to God. It is true that Adam is not reported to have brought an offering or a sacrifice, and for the first fifteen hundred years of the world's history there is no mention of a **Sin** Offering. The offerings were always burnt offerings (or possibly peace offerings also—see Exodus 24:5). And the spiritual significance of the two, as we will see in subsequent chapters, is widely different. We do not know that we are justified in making dogmatic statements as to why there is no reference to Sin Offerings prior to the Mosaic economy, but the explanation is probably to be found in the general principle which the Apostle lays down: that where there is no law there is no transgression. Sacrifices, however, were offered from the earliest times.

In the vision which Isaiah had as a young man he saw a throne set up in a temple, and Jehovah upon the throne. What throne was this if not the throne of the universe? And if the throne of the universe is set up in a temple, does it not indicate that those things for which the temple stood—mediation, access, worship, fellowship, that those spiritualities are, so to speak, the architectural lines upon which the universe is built?

We must not regard atonement and mediation as emergency measures which were resorted to in the presence of the exigency of sin. Are they not rather inherent in the very character of God? Did not the remedy for sin antedate the commission of sin? And the sacrificial system was God's method of bringing men to a gradual apprehension of the provision which was made in His very nature for the salvation of sinners.

We are thinking of the sacrificial system in this immediate connection in relation to its inward meanings and spiritual significance—as a possible or a positive means of grace. We are not overlooking the fact that it provided for a purely external approach to the outward symbols of revelation. It is this which the Writer of the Epistle to the Hebrews appears to have in mind when he speaks of the blood of bulls and goats, and the ashes of a heifer, when sprinkled upon the unclean, **sanctifying** to the purifying of the flesh *(Heb. 9:13)*. Quite apart from any spiritual dispositions that might be in exercise, the ritual was incumbent upon the people in making any outward approach to God, and to fail to observe it constituted disobedience; to refuse to do so was rebellion and anarchy. But we are keeping that in the background in the present enquiry.

What then are the fundamental ideas which are connected with sacrifices and offerings? What is at the heart of the sacrificial system? We suggest three things:

The first idea appears to be this: that God requires **the full devotion of the life.** In bringing the offering, the offerer brings something which represents himself, or which is in lieu of himself. But why does he bring an offering rather than present himself?

That question brings us to the second idea in the sacrificial system. **God requires that which is perfect.** And man knows that he cannot bring to God in his own person that which is perfect. The offering of sacrifices was the helpless acknowledgment that man

was unable to satisfy the requirements of a holy God,
who was looking for satisfaction of heart. The worshipper said, in effect; Do not look at me; I am sinful,
I am unworthy, I am unholy; look upon the gift; it
represents in symbol what I ought to be. That is
the second idea in the sacrificial system.

But there is something further than that. In bringing the offering man not only recognizes that God
requires the complete devotion of the life, and that he
has come short of the requirements of God: he acknowledges also that, in his shortcoming, he has forfeited his life. And thus it is that he must bring
something to die. This idea is not equally prominent
in all the offerings, but even in the Burnt Offering, in
which the prominent thought is devotion even unto
death, the vicarious element is present, for that devotion is lacking in man.

Now shall we see if we can move through the five
passages which we grouped together. The first one
was Hebrews 5:1.

When the Children of Israel came out from Egypt
they were a **redeemed** people. The passover blood
had saved them from the destruction which, in the
persons of the firstborn, had fallen· upon the entire
nation of Egypt. And it was for a redeemed people
that the sacrificial system was provided. And not only
were they a redeemed people, but the covenant into
which they entered at Sinai was ratified with blood.
This is alluded to in the Epistle to the Hebrews:

> "For when Moses had spoken every precept to all
> the people according to the Law, he took the blood of
> calves and of goats, with water, and scarlet wool, and
> hyssop, and sprinkled both the book, and all the peo-
> ple, saying, This is the blood of the testament which
> God hath enjoined unto you" *(Heb. 9:19,20)*.

It was not, therefore, the design of the sacrificial system to bring the Nation into covenant relationship with God, but rather to restore and maintain a broken communion. Nevertheless it enshrines and expresses such a breadth and variety of spiritual truth that we may well wonder whether there is any truth or aspect of truth in connection with the work of redemption which is not embodied in the symbolism of the "tabernacle of testimony" and the related ritual.

But the people, and particularly the more spiritually minded, recognized the inadequacy of these sacrifices in themselves to atone for sin, and indeed the transgressions from which there was **no justification** under the Law of Moses were numerous. There was, moreover no consistency in offering the sacrifices unless the act expressed a disposition upon the part of the worshipper. And thus it is that Micah cries out:

> "Will Jehovah be pleased with thousands of rams, or with ten thousands of rivers of oil"? (*Mic. 6:7, A. S. V.*).

The sacrifices, in so far as they might be a means of grace, were designed to **stimulate** spiritual dispositions, not to take their place. The sacrifices were a means, not an end. But in periods of spiritual declension they **took the place** of spiritual dispositions rather than expressed them. This is what Isaiah denounces in such stern reproofs:

> "What unto Me is the multitude of your sacrifices? saith Jehovah: I have had enough of the burnt-offerings of rams, and the fat of fed beasts; and I delight not in the blood of bullocks, or of lambs, or of he-goats. ** I cannot away with iniquity and the solemn meeting. ** And when ye spread forth your hands, I will hide Mine eyes from you; yea, when ye make many prayers, I will not hear: your hands are full of blood" (*Is. 1:11-15, A. S. V.*).

If the sacrifices had become an adjunct of iniquity they were worse than useless; they were blasphemy. If religion meant: sin and sacrifice; sin and sacrifice; they were prostituting the provisions of grace. You recall the appeal of the Apostle Paul, in the sixth chapter of Romans; shall we continue in sin that grace may abound? And you remember his reply: God forbid. There was a spiritual danger in connection with the sacrificial system which was similar, if not identical. If the offering up of sacrifices was divorced from those dispositions which it presupposed it was less than valueless, so far as the offerers of the sacrifices were concerned.

And so the·sacrificial system, as a means of grace, proved impotent, and had broken down, and God says, through Jeremiah:

"Put your burnt-offerings unto your sacrifices, and eat flesh" *(Jer. 7:21)*.

Do you see what God meant? The Burnt Offering was the offering of consecration: it was all burned on the altar, as representing the entire devotion of the life. The worshipper ate nothing of it, and the priest ate nothing of it. It expressed implicit obedience. But the offerings had become a sacred farce: they had no spiritual value or significance. They had become a spiritual anæsthetic; the national conscience was being drugged. Jeremiah is commissioned to say to them: "You may just as well finish the farce; eat your burnt offerings, and acknowledge that the whole performance is a profanity."

"For when I brought you out of Egypt, I said nothing about sacrifices, but I said, Obey My voice."

Then, where did sacrifices come in? They were designed, for those who could thus avail themselves of them, to restore and maintain communion between a

sinful people and a holy God. But the very offering
of them, even regarding them in their outward aspects
and from the lowest point of view, presupposed a
disposition to obey God, and if that were wanting it
was a hollow mockery.

Now, perhaps we are in a position to understand
something of what Jesus meant, when He said:

> "But go ye and learn what that meaneth, I will have
> mercy and not sacrifice".

He had been invited to a feast in Matthew's house,
and taxpayers and notorious sinners were the conspicuous guests. The feast was in honor of Jesus, and
Matthew invited the men whose company he would
appreciate. He was the **Friend** of sinners. He did
not tolerate them; He appreciated the opportunity of
mingling with them. And, perhaps, if possible, more
wonderful still, they appreciated Him. "There were
many", says the evangelist, "and they followed Him".

And when the Pharisees saw it, they said: "Why
eateth your Master with publicans and sinners"? And
when Jesus heard that, He said:

> "They that be whole need not a physician, but they
> that are sick. But go ye and learn what that meaneth,
> I will have mercy, and not sacrifice: for I am not come
> to call the righteous, but sinners to repentance".

That, in its inner meanings, is what the sacrificial
system was for. It was for people who were morally
sick. It was a means by which God could approach a
sinful people, and by which a sinful people could approach God. It was a "call" to sinners to repentance.
In His own person, Jesus **was** the sacrificial system:
He was the whole tabernacle ritual in flesh and blood.
And the declaration which He makes, in the words
of Hosea, is this:

> "I desire mercy and not sacrifice".

"Go ye", He says, "and learn what that meaneth". What **did** it mean?

Now do not become impatient if you do not understand the meaning of some of the sayings of Christ the first time that you hear them. The wisdom of the ages is hidden in them. He says: "Go and learn" what it means.

The whole sacrificial system was inaugurated because God wanted to have **mercy**. God was not enriched by the offerings. It was the method by which He sought to keep the flame of hope burning upon the altar of penitent hearts until One should come who could take away sin. You will find both of these thoughts expressed in the 50th Psalm.

"Hear, O My people, and I will speak; O Israel, and I will testify against thee: I am God, even thy God. I will not reprove thee for thy sacrifices or thy burnt-offerings, to have been continually before Me. I will take no bullock out of thy house, nor he goats out of thy folds. For every beast of the forest is Mine, and the cattle upon a thousand hills. I know all the fowls of the mountains: and the wild beasts of the field are Mine. If I were hungry I would not tell thee: for the world is Mine, and the fulness thereof. Will I eat the flesh of bulls, or drink the blood of goats? Offer unto God thanksgiving; and pay thy vows unto the Most High: and call upon Me in the day of trouble: I will deliver thee, and thou shalt glorify Me" (*vss. 7-15*).

That is the thought. I desire mercy and not sacrifice. Call upon Me and I will deliver thee. God desires to **exercise** mercy.

But there is another thought in this exclamation of the prophet. Having exhibited mercy Himself God desires to see mercy exhibited in the lives of those who have been the subjects of mercy. And this is what the prophet Micah was trying to say.

"Shall I come before Him with burnt offerings? * *
He hath shewed thee, O man, what is good; and what
doth the Lord require of thee, but to do justly, and to
love mercy, and to walk humbly with thy God"?

And so, when Jesus comes into the world, it is with
these words upon his lips: "Sacrifice and offering Thou
wouldest not, but a body hast thou prepared Me: * *
Lo, I come, * * to do Thy will, O God". Not sacrifice
but a body. But that body He presents as a sacrifice.

NOTE TO CHAPTER IV.

Questions may be raised as to why domestic animals
and the fruits of the ground were employed in sacrifices and offerings, and as to why the domestic animals
so used were confined to those animals which were
employed for food.

A German commentator goes, we think, to the heart
of these questions, when he says that man "offering
that which was the support of his life appeared thus
to offer the life itself."

This reasoning would apply equally to the domestic
animals which were used for food, and to the fruits
of the ground. The domestic animals and the fruits
of the ground were that upon which the worshipper
subsisted; they were, in symbol, as it were, his very
self. And that was the first idea in the sacrifice. The
offerer brought something which represented himself.

But if God, under the Mosaic economy, made a place
for bloodless sacrifices, why was He displeased with
the offering of Cain? Will you go back in your
thoughts to what was said with respect to the fundamental ideas at the heart of the sacrificial system?

(a) God requires the full devotion of the life. Cain's
offering acknowledges this. (b) God requires that

which is perfect.   And we may assume that Cain brought the best that he had, and recognized that also.   (c) But man has forfeited his life, and that is why he must bring something **to die**, and Cain did not acknowledge this.

CHAPTER V.

THE PASSOVER

THE history of the events which formed the background of the Egyptian passover are so familiar to every student of the Scriptures that it would seem to be unnecessary to even briefly recount it. The hour for deliverance from a long suffered and inexorible tyranny had at last arrived. The manner of its announcement by a messenger from a distant place, who had been specially commissioned of God, and the succession of judgments upon the people who enslaved them, were a witness to the oppressed Israelites that this deliverance was an answer to their cry to Heaven. God had heard. "I know their sorrows; and I am come down to deliver them * *".

It was in the crisis hour of this deliverance that the passover lamb was to be slain and the passover meal eaten. But the preparations were to be made and the meal partaken of before its accomplishment. They were thus called upon, in a spirit of faith, to anticipate what God had declared Himself about to do.

The preparations, moreover, were of a very deliberate character. Four days before the exodus each Israelitish household was to select a lamb: it was to be a male of the first year without blemish, taken from the sheep or from the goats. It was to be "kept up" from the tenth to the fourteenth day, and the whole assembly were to "kill it between the two evenings" (marg. A. S. V.).

The way in which these lambs are spoken of as if they constituted one composite sacrifice; the simultaneous act of putting them to death, and the formation of family and neighbour groups, mark it as a national sacrifice. Indeed, there was no provision for the cele-

bration of the passover by an individual Israelite. He
must form a group, with other like groups, and those
groups expressed a corporate idea.

It is a very striking fact that in connection with the
deliverance from Egypt, and even in the institution
of the passover ritual, there is no mention of sin or of
transgression or of any moral quality or delinquency.
God is not imputing trespasses to them. It may be
that one reason for this is to be found in the fact that
as a people they had not yet become the people of
God, and He had therefore no transgression to visit
upon them. Indeed, prior to the giving of the Law we
do not read of sin offerings, for by the law is the
knowledge of sin; and we do not read of trespass
offerings for where there is no law there is no transgression. And we notice, moreover, that the passover
sacrifice is in contrast to every sacrifice connected with
the tabernacle ritual. Those sacrifices spoke of consecration, of shortcoming, of transgression and sin.
The passover sacrifice corresponds to no one of the
tabernacle offerings. It is in a class by itself.

The passover lamb was not a burnt offering, nor a
meal offering, nor a peace offering, nor a sin offering,
nor a trespass offering. It was offered up, moreover,
without the mediation of a priest, and the intervention
of an altar. The blood was sprinkled, but it was with
the people's hands, and it was not beneath an altar
that it was poured, but it was sprinkled upon the
lintels and the doorposts of the homes.

The place of the passover, then, as a part of the sacrificial system of the Old Testament was unique. It
was to be observed year by year continually, but its
observance was to be as a "memorial". It commemorated the deliverance. And we think we may say
that henceforth it had no sacrificial value. It **was,**

however, to be offered at "the place which the Lord thy God shall choose", and the Nation seems to have interpreted this as requiring that the blood should be brought to the altar, for we read that they did so (*II Chron.* 30:16,17; 35:11,12). Nevertheless there is nothing in the Law specifically mentioning this. There is, however, nothing said as to the putting of the blood upon the doorposts in the memorial of the feast. The emphasis in the perpetual passover is upon the unleavened bread, which was to be eaten seven days.

The passover lamb was, we know, a type of Christ. "For even Christ, our passover", says the apostle, "is sacrificed for us". What aspect, then, of the sacrificial work of Christ does the passover lamb symbolize? If we would answer that question, we must look at the distinguishing character of the offering, and at the nature of the deliverance.

We have already observed that the passover sacrifice did not correspond to any one of the tabernacle offerings. Those offerings were not with the design, even symbolically, of bringing the people into covenant relationship with God, but rather of restoring and maintaining an impaired fellowship. Israel in the wilderness was already a redeemed people. And the passover lamb had signified and sealed that redemption. It had linked them to God as a united people in faith. And the blood expressed the cost at which deliverance is secured.

It was an hour of judgment upon Egypt; it was an hour of salvation for Israel. There was a clear line of cleavage between the two. The first-born of the Egyptians perished; the first-born of the Israelites were preserved. But the basis of the distinction was not the relative goodness of the two peoples. Whatever may have been the moral condition of the Egyptians we know that the Israelites were not all virtuous. And they were more or less given up to idolatry. Otherwise, how can we account for their lapse into the worship of a calf after the absence of Moses for forty days *(Ezek. 23:19)*?

Among the Egyptians not every man perished but the first-born only of every family, or in every home. And again, the discrimination was not upon moral grounds, for the eldest sons were not less worthy of mercy than the younger ones. How, then, are we to interpret the action of God? There may be that which we cannot fully understand, and it may become necessary to remind ourselves that God has eternity in which to work, and that His ways are past finding out. At times we can only exclaim with Abraham: "shall not the Judge of all the earth do right"?

But if the judgment on the one hand, and the salvation on the other, were not based upon moral discriminations, what was it that God was seeking to express and to bring about?

The character of God is revealed by the acts of God. We know what God is by what He is doing, by what He has done. In the last analysis, history will be found to have woven into its fabric the imprint of the signature of God. But in order to rightly appraise Divine actions we may need a measuring stick that stretches beyond the limit of this present life. And that not because "man is built on the scale of two worlds," though in respect to certain elements of his personality that may be true, but because God has come into human life, and in the death and resurrection of Christ related Himself to every rational soul. The hour is coming when "all that are in the graves shall hear His voice, and shall come forth". But would they ever come forth had not He?

The Egyptian passover with all of the related ante-
cedent and subsequent events was a living panorama
of spiritual truth. It not only marked an ever memo-
rable stage in Israel's history, it symbolized conflicts,
judgments and deliverances in spiritual spheres, and
in the souls of men.

When we consider the passover feast as a spiritual
drama, the first thing that impresses us is that there
are two companies. **All** the Egyptians constitute one
of these companies: **all** the Israelites constitute the
other. We said that the basis of the distinction was
not in the relative goodness of those who composed
the two peoples, and yet so skillfully is the Scripture
written, and with such wisdom are the events disposed,
that there is nevertheless a moral distinction between
the groups as a whole in that the Egyptians were op-
pressors and the Israelites were oppressed. And although there is no **virtue** in being oppressed, yet the
condition is one that calls for deliverance, and affords
the occasion for judgment upon the one and salvation
for the other.   And this is what the spiritual analogy
required.

On the one hand we see a company who are all the
subjects of judgment; on the other hand a company
who are all the subjects of deliverance. And this is
not because of individual merit and demerit, but rather
because the members of each group are bound together in the "bundle of life." There is an organic unity. And as we consider the analogy we see a vivid
portrayal in this historical setting of the declaration
of the apostle, millenniums afterwards, that as judgment came upon **all** men to condemnation, even so the
free gift came upon **all** men to justification of life.
"For all have sinned, and come short of the glory of
God": that is illustrated in the one company. "Being

justified freely by His grace": that is illustrated in the other company. And although, as we said before, there is no mention of sin or of transgression, nevertheless the Israelites, as well as the Egyptians, are under the sentence of death, else why should they have needed the protection of the passover blood? The ordinance becomes therefore a commentary upon the declarations of the Apostle that death passed upon all men, and death reigned from Adam to Moses (*Rom. 5:12-14*). And that which was already a fact is thus brought home to their consciences, and pictorially memorialized for the generations to come.

The Israelites were enjoined to strike the blood of the lambs upon the doorposts and lintels of their homes. Sin has become a question of life and death. "Without shedding of blood is no remission". But it is not **man's** blood that must be shed. God calls the passover "My sacrifice" (*Exo. 23:18; 34:25*). It is the Blood of Christ. And by putting the blood upon the outside of the house they advertized their faith; they openly declared their confidence.

But having thus done they withdrew into the house to feast upon the sacrifice.

And as they seek the shelter of the blood-sprinkled homes we notice three things:

1. Although they are feasting upon the lamb in perfect security, yet they are still in Egypt.

2. By their simultaneous action in the slaying of the lamb, and by their grouping of themselves together, they express a spiritual solidarity. They are one people.

3. Each housheld has a complete lamb—"a lamb for an house".

They are still in Egypt. Indeed they appear to have been surrounded by the Egyptians; to have been living in the midst of them. The narrative does not explain how this came to pass: the Egyptians may have been driven by fear, as the plagues followed one upon another, to the territory of the Israelites which was immune from some of them. That the Egyptians were about them is evidenced by their conduct in "spoiling" them as they went out.

But although the Israelites were indeed in Egypt they were a separated people. They were already a delivered people. They were sheltered behind shed blood. And that blood was the token to which God looked, for "when I see the blood", He had said, "I will pass over you".

And if Egypt is a symbol of this present evil world, then the spiritual analogy is intended to portray the believer as in the world, and yet not of it. In Egypt, and yet completely insulated by the blood, and feeding tranquilly upon the lamb.

And thus feeding, they express a spiritual solidarity. There are thousands of homes but upon the door of every home is the sprinkled blood, and within the doors of every house the assembled group is partaking of the offering. They are thus one people with a common faith and a mutual interest. From this hour they are a redeemed people; they have become as a people the people of God.

And each household has a complete lamb. There is a wonderful fact expressed in that provision of the ordinance. In the world and as yet on the threshold, as it were, of salvation every believer has a full Christ—a Christ to partake of and a Christ to share. Satisfaction and fellowship.

But they have already turned their backs upon Egypt: it is to be an alien country. They are never to return. Their loins are girded; they have shoes on their feet and their staff in their hand. They are ready to depart. There is indeed a certain impatience to be away; they eat it in haste.

They leave **Egypt** behind them but throughout all their generations they are to feed upon the **lamb**.

Israel had been saved. Henceforth, after they should reach the land, in the persons of their firstborn, they were to be dedicated to God. And in this connection a provision of the sacrificial system is brought into view. Every firstborn son, throughout their generations, was to be redeemed with a lamb. And this dedication extended to their cattle as well as to their sons. The original ordinance is given in the Book of Exodus:

> "And it shall be, when Jehovah shall bring thee into the land of the Canaanite, as He sware unto thee and to thy fathers, and shall give it thee, that thou shalt set apart unto Jehovah all that openeth the womb, and every firstling which thou hast that cometh of a beast; the males shall be Jehovah's. And every firstling of an ass thou shalt redeem with a lamb; and if thou wilt not redeem it, then thou shalt break its neck: and all the first-born of man among thy sons shalt thou redeem" *(Exod. 13:11-13, A. S. V.).*

The connection between this ordinance and the deliverance from Egypt is expressed in the context following:

> "And it shall be, when thy son asketh thee in time to come, saying, What is this? that thou shalt say unto him, By strength of hand Jehovah brought us out from Egypt, from the house of bondage: and it came to pass, when Pharaoh would hardly let us go, that Jehovah slew all the first-born in the land of Egypt, both the first-born of man, and the first-born of beast: therefore I sacrifice to Jehovah all that openeth the womb, being males; but all the first-born of my sons I redeem" *(Exod. 13:14, 15, A. S. V.).*

We return to the question of the special aspect of the work of Christ which the passover was intended to symbolize. When we consider that henceforth the people were a people of redemption and that, except commemoratively, the sacrifice was never repeated it assumes a very fundamental character. We have said that there was no mention of sin or transgression. The sacrifice seems to be too elemental for that. God is not discussing merit or demerit. He makes the all sufficient and all embracing sacrifice, and it avails for all. It avails completely. It is a finished work. God cannot **do** more: man cannot **need** more. He enjoins, therefore, upon every Israelite to take the lamb, to sprinkle the blood, to keep the feast. But it is eaten with unleavened bread, for although redemption does not wait upon merit as a contributing cause, it looks to separation from evil as an ensuing consequence. And leaven must be put away as they feed upon the lamb.

The passover sacrifice, therefore, is altogether in a class by itself. The blood was placed by the Israelites upon the doorposts for one purpose and one only—to save them from death. In the persons of the firstborn the entire Egyptian people came representatively under the power of death. And that same doom was at Israel's door.

But there must surely be a meaning in the fact that it was only **representatively** that the carrying out of the sentence affected the Egyptian nation as a whole. Actually the nation was preserved. And in as much as it is one of the outstanding events in the history of redemption, it must be intended to teach fundamental truth as to God's dealing with the world. There was a visitation of judgment; a sentence of death. But "how unsearchable are His judgments, and His ways past finding out"! For it is of that same nation that we read long afterwards the Lord of Hosts shall one day say: "Blessed be Egypt My people" *(Is. 19:25)*.

What a picture is this that Isaiah draws! He sees a "triple alliance" under the special blessing of God. The two great foes of Israel had been Egypt and Assyria. The menace was first from one and then from the other. But here in the prophetic vision of the Seer they stand on either side as covenant allies. And whether we take the prophecy as substantial or metaphorical, the underlying spiritual principle is the same. **Egypt is blessed.** And however substantial the prophecy may be we can hardly escape from the implications of analogy. "God sent not His Son into the **world** to condemn the **world**; but that the **world** through Him might be saved".

NOTE TO CHAPTER V.

There was a requirement in connection with the sacrificial system which while not directly connected with the passover memorial yet by an association of ideas finds suitable mention here. The annual passover sacrifice celebrated the deliverance, in the person of the firstborn, of the entire Israelitish nation from death. The **dedication** of the firstborn continually reminded the people, family by family, that whereas the firstborn in every Egyptian family had been cut off, **their** firstborn had been preserved. But there was another ordinance in which every individual child was brought into remembrance before God. Every Israelitish mother was required to bring a burnt offering and a sin offering after the birth of each child. This ordinance is found in the twelfth chapter of Leviticus. And while the childbirth sacrifices were not in the nature of a redemption for the child but of a purification for the mother, yet the emphasis upon the burnt offering in this ordinance suggests a dedication of the mother on behalf of the child.

The mother's **childbirth** offering might be two turtles or two pigeons if she were not able to bring a lamb. Both of these requirements are alluded to in the Gospel narrative *(Luke 2:22-24).*

CHAPTER VI.

THE FIVE OFFERINGS

IF the sacrificial ritual of the Old Testament has no symbolic or typical significance it is perhaps almost waste of time to pursue a study of it, but if it has such significance, then it is a study which is little less than profound.

In the closing chapter of the Book of Exodus the tabernacle is reared. In the opening sentence of the Book of Leviticus God speaks to Moses "out of the tabernacle"! God had spoken before. His voice had been heard by the people from Mount Sinai, and He had communed there with Moses face to face. The people had been unspeakably awed by the presence of God. It had been a terrible experience. The summit of the mountain had presented the aspect of a smoking caldron; the phenomena are described as fire and blackness and darkness and tempest and the sound of a trumpet and the voice of words which those who heard it could not endure. And so terrible was the sight that even Moses said: I exceedingly fear and quake.

But God had now surrounded Himself with the symbols of redemption which made it possible for Him to dwell among a rebellious and disobedient people. Symbolically the sacrificial system was the way back, albeit of a redeemed people, into fellowship with God.

In the first seven chapters of Leviticus we have a recital of five classes of sacrifices or oblations, together with a section devoted to the "law of the offerings".

In the five offerings we have five aspects of the atoning work of Christ, for it is manysided, and cannot be symbolized fully in any one offering. In a similar way there are given us in the Gospel records four aspects of His **person**. Here in the offerings there are five aspects of His **work**.

There is a spiritual significance in numbers. In the number one we have the ideas of unity, of primacy, of supremacy, of sovereignty. God is one. But there is also the idea of a solitary exclusiveness. And the full revelation of God is not connected with the number one. The God of revelation is a triune God.

In the number two we have more than one. It at once introduces a new element, an element which may bring in either harmony or discord, unity or enmity.

In the number three we have the first guarantee of harmony, either by suppression or unanimity, by consent or constraint. It suggests also completeness; the manifestation of the Godhead is of a threefold character. It suggests also solidarity. The cube is the expression of this idea; the length and the breadth and the height of it are equal.

In the number four we have the idea of universality —the four corners of the earth, the four winds of heaven. But there is also the suggestion of weakness. This is illustrated in the human hand. How helplessly impotent the four fingers are without the thumb!

In the number **five** there seems to be the idea of responsibility according to the measure of capacity. And we look at the human hand again. The hand is the instrument of accomplishment—so much so that we speak of industrial laborers as "hands." But man cannot do much with only **one** hand, and so five suggests a limited capacity, a capacity that has been curtailed. And that is where man finds himself. He is half impotent on account of sin. And so it is that when we, as it were, turn the coin over we have in the number five the number of **grace**. God's provision to cover man's responsibility. And if this be so it is suitable indeed that there should be five offerings to represent the atoning work of Christ.

But not only the **number** of the offerings, but the **order** in which they are recited has spiritual suggestiveness. The arrangement expresses the work of atonement from the Divine point of view, and exhibits, as it were, God coming out to man. Had the arrangement been intended to express man's approach to God the trespass offering would have been placed first, and the burnt offering last. This will be appreciated more fully as we study the characteristics of the offerings individually.

The Burnt Offering is the first one in order. It was a living sacrifice; it was offered, as the margin has it, "for acceptance", and it was all consumed upon the altar. It was this latter characteristic that was the distinguishing feature; it was **all for God**. It was the offering of entire devotion.

The Meal Offering, which is next in order, was **not** a living sacrifice. It was of flour, or corn, anointed with oil, and with frankincense sprinkled upon it. There was also added some salt. This offering was not all for God: there was a portion for God—a sweet savor, but the major portion was eaten by Aaron and his sons. This offering, then, was for **God and the priests**.

The Peace Offering is the central one of the five. It was a living sacrifice but, except for the fat, it was not consumed on the altar. This offering was shared in by the **offerer**, by the **priests**, and by **God**. It was thus outstandingly the offering of fellowship, of communion.

The Sin Offering and the Trespass Offering more nearly approach one another than the other offerings. In the **Sin** Offering we have sin in its nature, sin in the abstract. In the **Trespass** Offering we have the overt

act, the transgression. But the section dealing with
the Sin Offering passes over into the section dealing
with the Trespass Offering with such indefiniteness
that it is difficult for some to determine where the one
terminates and the other begins. The whole of Lev.
5 (but particularly vss. 14-19) forms a kind of bridge
between the one section and the other. It is even so
in experience. The dividing line between sin and sins
is too indistinct for ordinary spiritual apprehension to
discern, or to concern itself with.

It was stated that the Peace Offering was the central
one. This is so in the detailed statement of the offerings, but when we come to the section which gives
"the law of the offerings" the order is changed and the
Peace Offering is brought in at the end. The significance attaching to the arrangements will be seen when
we study the offerings individually, and in their relation one to the other.

NOTE TO CHAPTER VI.

In bringing these offerings into the presence of God,
the offerer was, in symbol, presenting to God that with
which God could be completely satisfied, and by laying his hands upon the offering he identified himself
with it.

The Rabbis mention five acts as belonging to the
offerer of a sacrifice:

1. The laying on of hands
2. Slaying
3. Skinning
4. Cutting up
5. Washing the inwards.

There were also five priestly functions:

1. Catching up the blood

2. Sprinkling it
3. Lighting the altar fire
4. Laying on the wood
5. Bringing up the pieces, as well as all else done at the altar itself.

Every offering was accompanied by prayer. The following was the prayer used in offering private sacrifices:

"I entreat, O Jehovah, I have sinned; I have done perversely; I have rebelled; I have committed * * (naming the sin); but I return in repentance, and let this be for my atonement."

Every offering was, of course a type of Christ, as to some aspect of His person and work, and the idea of expiation was recognized by the synagogue. Edersheim quotes this from one of the Jewish writers:

"The soul of every creature is bound up in its blood; therefore I gave it to atone for the soul of man—that one soul should come and atone for the other."

CHAPTER VII.

THE ALTARS

IN connection with the Mosaic ritual there were two
altars, one of which was outside the tabernacle,
and the other within. On one of them there were
offered up sacrifices: on the other sacrifices were not
offered. At the one any priest might minister: to the
other the high priest only might approach. The one
was the altar of burnt offering; the other was the altar
of incense. There was also what we might speak of
as an improvised altar outside the Camp.

On the altar of burnt offering, morning and evening,
year in and year out, there was offered up a lamb for
a burnt offering. On special occasions other burnt
offerings were presented. And individual Israelites
might at any time bring a burnt offering.

In addition to the burnt offerings there were offered
on this altar portions of the meal offerings which were
called the "memorial". These were, so to speak, adjuncts of the burnt offerings. In addition to the burnt
offerings, and the memorial of the meal offerings, there
were also offered certain portions of the peace offerings, of the sin offerings and of the trespass offerings.
But those portions seem to have constituted the burnt
offering portions of those offerings, so that we think
it may be said that no offerings other than burnt
offerings were offered upon that altar.

This is clearly implied in the ritual of the Sin Offering. Should the worshipper find himself unable to
bring the prescribed sacrificial animal he might, as
an alternative, offer a pair of turtle doves or two young
pigeons. In such a case, one of the two birds was to
be offered as a burnt offering. This seems to be a

clear indication that a part of the Sin Offering was regarded as a Burnt Offering *(Lev. 5:7; 12:8)*.

The Altar of Burnt Offering is sometimes spoken of as a type of the Cross. We question whether it is appropriate to refer to the altars as types; they are rather symbols than types. But it would seem that if the Altar of Burnt Offering was intended to be a symbol of the Cross of Christ it must have been so in a restricted sense, and with reference to certain aspects only of His vicarious work. The Sin Offerings were not brought to it, and no sinner, as such, might approach to it. Even the "Levites" were disqualified from the service of the altar: this was reserved for the priests; and they appear to have represented "the worshipper idealized." Moreover, it was the Godward aspect of the work of Christ, and we think we may say it was this exclusively, that found expression in the sacrifices that were brought to this altar.

What then did the sacrificial altars symbolize? For the things which are seen in the Altar Ritual are figures of the unseen; they are material expressions of spiritual realities. What, we ask, is it that occurs at these altars? It was there that the sacrifices were brought. They were **laid** on the altar, and those sacrifices that were to be consumed were consumed there. It was there that God and man met. It was at the altar that God entered into the sacrifice. Do we not then come as nearly to the heart of the symbolism as we may if we think of the sacrificial altars as the heart of God? Where was the sacrifice of Calvary really made? Was it not in the heart of God? God was "in Christ" reconciling the world unto Himself. But if we are to look for a suggestion of the Cross of Christ it would seem to be rather at the place outside the Camp where the Sin Offerings were burned. The

Writer of the Epistle to the Hebrews speaks of this altar. He says:

"We have an altar, whereof they have no right to eat which serve the tabernacle" *(Heb. 13:10).*

If we ask: to what altar does he refer? the next verse seems to answer the question.

"For the bodies of those beasts, whose blood is brought into the sanctuary by the high priest for sin, are burned without the camp".

These were the Sin Offerings for the Nation, or for the high priest. The blood of no other offerings was taken into the Holy Place. And those sacrifices were not partaken of by the priests.

There was then, as it were, an improvised altar outside the Camp. Why was this? The Camp of Israel was sanctified by the presence of Jehovah. The Sin Offering expressed the essence of sin. It was a polluted thing; as such it was removed from the presence of God. But it was, nevertheless, a sacred thing, for it was a type of Christ "made * * sin for us". And it was to be taken to a **clean place.**

"Wherefore", he says, "Jesus also, that He might sanctify the people with His own Blood, suffered without the gate". He was crucified outside the walls. He was led there. But the Writer speaks of it as a voluntary act. What was the significance? Suppose that the Sin Offering had been consumed **within** the Camp, would it not have seemed to imply that the death of the Messiah was only and exclusively for Israel? The Sin Offering was taken outside the Camp of Israel. It was not consumed on Israel's altar.

And so when Jesus offered Himself as the Sin Offering for the whole world He went outside the Camp. There is a meaning in that for Israel and for us. We do not have to become Jews in order to become Christians, but an Israelite does have to forsake the religious communion in which he was reared, and to go forth voluntarily outside the Camp.

Of that altar, which was without the Camp, of the sacrifices which were offered there, the Israelite had no right to partake. Those sacrifices represented the wage of sin; in those sacrifices we see Christ, as made sin for us, abandoned by God. And all that was left of the sacrifices was ashes. There was nothing in that which could offer spiritual nourishment. Moreover those Sin Offerings for the whole nation were Godward rather than manward, and satisfied Divine righteousness rather than human need. The Nation did not enter into that.

But the Writer implies that we **have** a right to eat, even of that altar. In the offering consumed without the Camp we have an **aspect** of the redemptive work of Christ. But Christ Himself is not divided. And He came out to us that we might partake of Him. He has turned death into life; He has overcome death by suffering death, and **the altar which was a table of pollution He has turned into a festal board.**

But notice vss. 14 and 15 of that 13th chapter of Hebrews:

"For here we have no continuing city, but we seek one to come. By Him therefore let us offer the sacrifice of praise to God continually, that is, the fruit of our lips, giving thanks to His Name".

Having renounced the earthly Jerusalem they have a Heavenly City. And having left behind the sacrificial system of the Old Covenant they find themselves enjoying a new liberty in offering up spiritual sacrifices. Yes, and there is another spiritual sacrifice mentioned in the sentence following:

"But to do good and to communicate forget not: for with such sacrifices God is well pleased".

We have spoken more particularly of the altar of burnt offering and of the improvised altar, if we may so designate it, outside the Camp. There is little doubt that that improvised altar was in direct line eastward with the altar of burnt offering. The altar of burnt offering, on the other hand, was in direct line with the altar of incense. The altar of incense was in the holy place without the veil which hung between the holy place and the holiest of all. On that altar incense was offered up by the high priest morning and night. The incense symbolized the people's prayers. But the thought of vicarious sacrifice is there also, for the blood is taken there from the altar of burnt offering. And here, as prevailing prayer is offered as sweet incense, we have at this inner altar also the movements of the heart of God.

We have said that no sacrifices were presented on the altar of incense. There was, however, a close and vital connection between that altar and the altar of burnt offering. What was that connection?

Notice that before the high priest offered his daily incense at the altar of incense there had been offered up the daily burnt offering on the altar of burnt offering. Had not Christ presented a life of complete devotion on earth, He could not have exercised an effectual ministry in Heaven. Moreover the **fire** which consumed the incense was taken from the altar of burnt offering. And observe also that the altar of burnt offering was where every Israelite could see it, whereas the altar of incense was where no one could see it but the priests, and that not without entering the tent. It would seem then that what was done at the altar of Burnt Offering symbolized what Christ was, and what Christ did, in the presence of men, and that what was done at the altar of incense symbolized what Christ is, and what Christ does, in the presence of God. At the altar of burnt offering we see Christ on earth: at the altar of incense we see Christ in Heaven.

There is undoubtedly a spiritual significance in the fact that the Writer of the Epistle to the Hebrews speaks of the altar of incense as pertaining to the Holiest of All. Its position in the Holy Place was a contrivance of grace, by way of accommodation in order that the high priest might make a daily approach, and at the same time to give continual witness to the fact that the way into the holiest was not yet made manifest.

But if we would get the full thought in connection with the altar of incense we must draw aside the veil. We may see this more fully in a subsequent study.

CHAPTER VIII.

THE BLOOD

THE sacredness of blood is in that it is the seat of life. And the higher the form of life the more sacred the blood in which it resides. Man's blood cannot therefore be shed with impunity, for "in the image of God made He man". And so it is written: "Whoso sheddeth man's blood, by man shall his blood be shed" *(Gen. 9:6)*. The **eating** of blood, moreover, was forbidden under penalty of death, and this on a twofold ground. For not only was it the seat of life; it was also the accepted means of atonement. It had thus a double sacredness. "For the life of the flesh is in the blood: and I have given it to you upon the altar to make an atonement for your souls: for it is the blood that maketh an atonement for the soul" *(Lev. 17:11)*. Only life can atone for life. We are therefore "made nigh by the Blood of Christ" *(Eph. 2:13)*, for He "made peace through the Blood of His Cross" *(Col. 1:20)*; and we have "redemption through His Blood, even the forgiveness of sins" *(Col. 1:14)*, for "by His own Blood He entered in once into the holy place, having obtained eternal redemption" *(Heb. 9:12)*.

We may be quite sure therefore that there will be significance attaching to every requirement and regulation as to the presentation of the blood in the sacrificial system. And yet, on the other hand, we may expect simplicity, for here, if anywhere, God desires to be understood.

The Egyptian passover sacrifice being the initial ordinance we may look there not only for simplicity but for that which is elemental as well.

The blood of this sacrifice was to be sprinkled with hyssop, which was an unpretentious shrub. It was to be put on the sideposts and the upper doorposts of the dwelling doors, so that those who entered should be enveloped by it. But thus placed it was a "token", so that they were shielded through it. And the value of it was according to God's estimate, so that when He saw the blood He would save from judgment every sheltered home. But the blood thus sprinkled was not only a token to God; it was also a witness to men, for it advertized the faith in the Word of God of those who sprinkled it.

When we come to the priestly ritual the requirements are still simple as to that which is to be done; nothing can be misunderstood: the spiritual meanings, however, are deeper.

In the first place, although the worshipper slays the sacrifice, only the priest may present the blood. A sinner, as such, cannot bring the atoning blood to God. He may only stand and look as the blood is presented by one whom God has qualified to make the approach.

In presenting the blood it was variously:

    (a) Poured out at the base of the altar of burnt offering *(Exod. 29:12; Lev. 4:7)*.

    (b) Sprinkled round about upon the altar of burnt offering *(Lev. 1:5; Exod. 29:16, 20)*.

    (c) Sprinkled **on** the altar of burnt offering *(Exod. 24:6)*.

    (d) Put upon the horns of the altar of burnt offering *(Exod. 29:12)*.

    (e) Put upon the horns of the altar of incense *(Exod. 30:10; Lev. 4:7)*.

    (f) Sprinkled before Jehovah *(Lev. 4:6)*.

    (g) Sprinkled upon the mercy seat and before the mercy seat *(Lev. 16:14, 15)*.

    (h) Sprinkled directly before the tabernacle of the congregation *(Num. 19:4)*.

In applying the blood to man, it was:

(a) Sprinkled on the people *(Exod. 24:8).*

(b) Sprinkled on the priests *(Exod. 29:21; Lev. 8:30).*

(c) Put on the tip of the right ear, thumb and great toe of Aaron and of his sons *(Exod. 29: 20; Lev. 8:24).*

(d) Sprinkled upon the leper at the time of his cleansing, and likewise upon a house that was cleansed from leprosy *(Lev. 14:4-7, 49-51).*

Each of these actions had its own significance.

There was a disposition made of the blood in one instance, however, in which it was consumed in the fire, except as to a portion of it which was sprinkled before the tabernacle. This was the case in connection with the sacrifice of the red heifer, the ashes of which were employed for the water of purification. The sprinkled blood, however, was not taken into the presence of God, nor even to the altar of burnt offering, but was sprinkled at the place of sacrifice in the direction of the tent. This singular disposition of the blood would seem to express an intense activity of judgment in which the utter displeasure of God can find no satisfaction in the atoning sacrifice, but must consume relentlessly that which has become an offense.

It is a striking fact, however, that the sacrifice in which there is this consumption of the blood by the fire is not the "sin offering", but is a sacrifice which is in a category by itself, and is undesignated by any name attaching to the five orders of offerings. In this it resembles the passover sacrifice.

It was only in the case of sin offerings that the blood was poured out at the base of the altar of burnt offering, and inasmuch as the altar of burnt offering was the symbol of fellowship the blood thus poured out bore witness to the fact that it was the **foundation** of fellowship with God. It was also, except in the case of a sin offering for the high priest or the congregation, put upon the **horns** of this altar, for the fellowship thus created is something far more than restored intercourse. There is in fellowship between God and man an element of energized activity as symbolized by the horns. Man is brought into fellowship with God for service as well as for companionship. The horns are the symbols of power. And all effective aggressiveness in the domain of the Spirit is related to the shed blood. "They overcame him by the Blood of the Lamb" *(Rev. 12:11)*.

We said that some of the blood of the sin offerings was put upon the horns of the altar of burnt offering except in the case of sin offerings for the anointed priest or for the congregation. In these cases the priest dipped his finger in the blood and sprinkled of the blood seven times before Jehovah, before the veil of the sanctuary. The priest then put some of the blood upon the horns of the altar of sweet incense. It was at this altar that the high priest exercised his special ministry, and the need of atonement is acknowledged at the place of service.

There was indeed another exception to the putting of the blood of the sin offering upon the horns of the altar of burnt offering, but this exception appears to have symbolized the meager spiritual apprehension of the worshipper who was not able to bring any other offering than birds. In this case the blood was sprinkled on the **side** of the altar.

The disposition of the blood in the case of burnt offerings and peace offerings and trespass offerings was different from that of sin offerings. The blood of these sacrifices was sprinkled "round about upon the altar". Those spiritualities for which these sacrifices stood were thus identified with atonement, but from a different point of view. If in the sin offering the blood is seen to be the **basis** of fellowship, it may be that in these other offerings the blood is the **bond** of fellowship. In the one the blood is poured out at the altar's base; in the other the blood is sprinkled round about.

In connection with the ratification of the covenant at Sinai the blood was sprinkled by Moses "on the altar" (*Exod. 24:6*). This was before the tabernacle ritual had been inaugurated and the thought is more general in its character, but an altar is there and the blood is applied.

Now all that is done at the altar of burnt offering is done in the sight of men. But there is a satisfaction rendered by the Blood of Christ into which man cannot enter, and in which the throne of God is exclusively concerned. This has already been expressed in the sin offerings for the high priest and the congregation in that the blood was sprinkled in the holy place, and upon the altar of incense, rather than on the altar of burnt offering. Even this, however, took place on the manward side of the veil. It was only on the annual Day of Atonement that the blood was taken within the veil, and sprinkled upon the mercy seat. And the sacrifices whose blood was thus taken to the throne of God, although as to the one, selected by the high priest, and as to the other, taken from the congregation, were an expression of God's recognition of atonement rather than of a consciousness of need in the heart of man.

There was, however, in the sacrificial system an

application of the blood to man as well as a presentation of the blood to God.

When the covenant at Sinai was first entered into we read that Moses reared an altar under the Mount and sent young men who offered burnt offerings and peace offerings. Moses then took half of the blood, and put it into basons and half of the blood, as already observed, he sprinkled on the altar *(Exod. 24:6)*. There was in this application of the blood a recognition of a twofold efficacy. It was sprinkled upon the altar: it was sprinkled upon the people.

In the sacrificial system the altar would seem to represent the heart of God. There is a moral necessity in the heart of God which must be met. He must express Himself freely and fully in the presence of moral delinquency. His righteousness and His love must both find full expression. But inasmuch as sin is in the nature of a revolt there must be a **triumphant** element in the exhibition of grace. All this is symbolized by the blood. It witnesses to the unmeasured love of God, for His life is laid down: it speaks of His righteousness for His life was laid down as an expiation for sin. But the blood also testifies to a triumph over death, which is the wages of sin, for it is as a symbol of life that the blood is sprinkled upon the altar.‡

But the same blood that is sprinkled upon the altar is sprinkled upon the people. There is perhaps nothing in all the sacrificial ritual which is more impressive than this. The garments of the people are **stained** with blood. And when Aaron and his sons are set apart to the priest's office they and their garments are sprinkled with the atoning blood. And that same blood is already on the tip of their right ears; upon the

‡See Note at end of chapter.

thumb of their right hands and upon the great toe of their right feet. The priests and the people are thus identified with all that which is symbolized by the blood. They are "marked men." This is the insignia of the saints. The people of God are blood sprinkled because they are blood bought. And they are blood bought because they could be purchased in no other way. How humbling, and yet how dignifying is this sprinkled blood. It is humbling for it speaks of condemnation: it is dignifying for it speaks of the Divine estimate of that which is redeemed. And it is inspiring, for it testifies to devotion unto death; of love to the uttermost. It speaks of the Cross, for it was there that the Blood was shed, but it speaks of the throne, for it is there that the Blood is taken as the perpetual token of a finished work and a final victory.

The sin offering was taken outside the Camp, and Jesus that He might sanctify the people with His own Blood suffered without the gate. The Blood has been shed for the whole world. But the blood is sprinkled upon the household of faith. The leper was not sprinkled with the blood until he had been pronounced "clean". The priests were sprinkled as consecrated men: the congregation was sprinkled as a seal of their covenant vows. They may indeed break their covenant, but His covenant is sure, and He is the Everlasting God.

NOTE TO CHAPTER VIII.

Is the blood a symbol of life or a symbol of death? If we look at the significance of the sacrificial system as a whole, it would seem that we must reach the conclusion that the blood was a symbol of life, not of

death. The altar was the table of Jehovah. Would
that which was a symbol of death have been sprinkled
upon and about the table of God? But it may be said
that the blood was not living blood. That is true.
And that fact gives it its sacrificial value: it was a type
of the Blood of **Christ**. He laid down His life, yet it
was not taken from Him, and He had power to take
it again. The blood then which is sprinkled upon
the altar, and which is taken into the presence of God,
must be regarded as pulsating with resurrection life.

In contrast to this, it would seem that the ashes are
the symbol of death. What is done with the ashes?
They fall through the grating of the altar, and are
gathered up with reverent care. The procedure is
given in the sixth chapter of Leviticus under the "law
of the burnt-offering". It reads thus:

> "The priest shall put on his linen garment, and his
> linen breeches shall he put upon his flesh, and he shall
> take up the ashes whereto the fire hath consumed the
> burnt-offering on the altar, and he shall put them be-
> side the altar. And he shall put off his garments, and
> put on other garments, and carry forth the ashes with-
> out the camp unto a clean place" *(A. S. V.)*.

Why this scrupulous ceremonial care? They represent that in Jesus which was consumed in devotion
to God: they are the emblems of the burnt out consecration of Christ.

That the ashes were the symbol of death seems to
be implied in the nineteenth chapter of Numbers in
connection with a ceremony of which we shall speak
in detail in a subsequent chapter. He who was appointed to gather the ashes of the sacrifices there described should be "unclean until the even" *(Num.*
19:10).

CHAPTER IX.

THE FIRE

A FEATURE of the sacrificial system, which in the nature of the case was essential to it, and yet was in a way apart from it, was the **FIRE**. It may be that sufficient attention has not been given to the spiritual significance attaching to this element in general, and to its place in the sacrificial ritual in particular.

We cannot read the Scriptures attentively without observing the repeated instances in which some quality in the Godhead, or some spiritual activity, is expressed by the representation, or by the actual operation, of fire.

In Genesis 3:24 we read that God placed at the east of the Garden of Eden Cherubims and a **flaming** sword. In Exodus 3:2-6 the Angel of Jehovah appears to Moses **in a flame of fire** out of the midst of a bush, and God called unto him **out of the midst of the bush**. In Exodus 19:18-20 we read of Mount Sinai being altogether on a smoke because **Jehovah** descended upon it **in fire**. In Exodus 24:15-17 it is said that the cloud covered the Mount, and the glory of Jehovah abode upon Mount Sinai, and the **sight** of the glory of Jehovah was like **devouring fire** on the top of the Mount. In Deuteronomy 4:36 Moses reminds the people that Jehovah caused them "to hear His voice", and had showed them **His great fire**, and that they had heard His words **out of the midst of the fire**. In Deuteronomy 9:3 Moses tells the people that Jehovah will destroy their enemies **as a consuming fire**. In Judges 13:20, as Manoah and his wife look on, the Angel of Jehovah ascends **in the flame of the altar**. In Second Chronicles 7:1 we read that when Solomon had made an end of praying **the fire** came down from heaven and consumed the burnt offering and the sacrifices; and the glory of Jehovah filled the house. In the 1st chapter of Ezekiel the prophet has a vision of the **glory of Jehovah**. In the 4th verse he sees **a fire** infolding itself and brightness proceeds **out of the midst of the fire**. In the 27th verse similar language is used, and in the 28th verse he says that this was the appearance of **the glory of Jehovah**. In Malachi 3:2 the prophet says that Jehovah is like a **refiner's fire**. In Hebrews 12:29 the Writer speaks of God as a **consuming fire**.

These allusions express some quality in God. What, then, are the qualities and what is the action of fire? What was the significance of the burning of the offerings?

It should be remembered at the very outset that it is not the action of the fire that makes the atonement: the shedding of the blood accomplishes this. The action of the fire is something apart. And furthermore, the consuming agent did not inhere in the sacrifice: the sacrifice did not **burn itself** out. The burning was the operation of an agent outside of itself. And there was one offering, and this the foundation sacrifice, which was not burned. There was no burning in connection with the passover sacrifice (except as some portion should remain until the morning). It would seem, then, that the burning, whatever its significance, was **within the area of redemption**. For, as we have seen in a previous chapter, the passover sacrifice brought the entire people into the sphere of redemption through faith, and the tabernacle ritual could not therefore have been designed to do this.

One of the prominent thoughts in connection with the action of the fire is undoubtedly that of judgment. Even a superficial reading of the Scriptures makes this impression upon the mind. We read in the Book of

Leviticus concerning Nadab and Abihu, "there came forth fire from before Jehovah and devoured them" *(Lev. 10:2, A. S. V.)*. "A fire goeth before Him", the Psalmist says, "and burneth up His enemies round about" *(Ps. 97:3)*. "His rebuke", says Isaiah, is "with flames of fire" *(Is. 66:15)*. We are told in the Book of Numbers that the fire of Jehovah burned among the people and consumed them *(Num. 11:1)*. And again, it is said that there came out a fire from Jehovah and devoured the two hundred and fifty men of Korah's company *(Num. 16:35)*. In Abraham's day a group of cities suffered the judgment of fire.

Judgment, however, is not the only thought connected with fire, for it carries to Heaven the fragrance of the "sweet savour offerings", and, moreover, if the fire is within the sphere of redemption, the judgment would be within that sphere also.

We should be exceedingly guarded in interpreting the significance of symbols and types, that we do not build doctrines upon insecure foundations at the suggestion of some feature of an ordinance that is obscure or incidental, and to which we may apply a meaning that is unwarranted. But where a symbol is repeatedly employed in the Scripture, from the beginning to the end, we should be able to receive clear spiritual instruction from an attentive contemplation of the occasions in which it is employed, the manner of its action, and its setting in relation to other symbols and spiritualities. If, then, we would seek the spiritual meaning of the fire in connection with the sacrificial system, our attention should fasten itself particularly upon those offerings which were the special subjects of it. These were: the Sin Offerings for the high priest, or for the nation as a whole, the "red heifer" offering, and the Burnt Offerings. These sacrifices, and these

only, were completely consumed, save that the **skin**
of a burnt offering was retained by the priest *(Lev. 7:
8).*

The Sin Offerings emphasized the thought of innate
depravity and spiritual helplessness: the "red heifer"
offering, as we shall see in a subsequent chapter, was
specially identified with the fact of death, and the
burnt offerings were the symbol of devotedness.

The **action** of the fire in the case of these offerings is
identical. The significance, however, may be different
in the one and in the other, although in each the fire
ascends and takes with it, as it were, the sacrifice.

It had been said in the beginning: "in the day that
thou eatest thereof, thou shalt surely die". The wages
of sin was death. And the Law was in keeping with
this, in that the most grievous offences were punishable with death. This was the extreme penalty. In
presenting a Sin Offering the worshipper, as we have
seen, brought as an expiation **something to die**. He
slew it with his own hand. What, then, was the significance of the subsequent burning of the offering? Why
did not the forfeiture of the life suffice?

We recognize, in the nature of things, some disposition must needs have been made of the carcases. To
have permitted decomposition would have been a
sacrilege; to have buried them would manifestly have
been unfit. To consume them was perhaps the inevi-
table alternative. But it was in obedience to something
more than a mere necessity that this was done. The
burning was an altar ministry. It was a part of the
ritual. And as such we may well inquire into its spiritual significance.

The action of the fire in consuming the sin offerings
may have a twofold significance. In the slaying of the
sacrifice the offerer has already acquiesced in, and

submitted to, the judgment of God, for in the case of every offering it was assumed that it was voluntarily brought, whether by an individual Israelite, or by the nation as a whole. And, ideally, it **must** express this if it is to be a true type of Christ. But in the burning of the sacrifice man is not only brought into a participation with the moral dispositions of God; there is an active fellowship set up, as it were, between man and God.

But the judgment so symbolized is an expression of holy wrath. The fire consumes that which is offensive to God. Nevertheless the fire ascends to God, for Christ has identified Himself with that which God has condemned. He has been made sin, and the fire carries the sin offering to heaven.

The offering of the "red heifer" would seem to come in the category of the sin offerings, but there is an even more intense activity of judgment than in the offerings so named. There is no blood taken to the altar and, except for that which is sprinkled in the direction of the tent, even the blood is consumed in the fire. But there **was** a sprinkling of blood; the blood was not **all** consumed. Otherwise the burning might express hopelessness; a satisfaction to God indeed, but no salvation for man.

In the case of the Burnt Offering the fire ascends from the altar, and the sacrifice is a "sweet savour". It takes with it the essence and aroma of the sacrifice. This is what the apostle alludes to when he says:

"Walk in love, as Christ also hath loved us, and hath given Himself for us an offering and a sacrifice to God for a sweet-smelling savour" (*Eph. 5:2*).

It was this offering that was presented day by day, morning and evening, continually. It was a perpetual sacrifice. And it would seem that, strictly speaking,

no other sacrifice than this was brought to the altar.
Indeed the altar was **designated** "the altar of burnt-
offering". Those **portions** of offerings, other than
burnt offerings, that were brought to this altar, seem
to have symbolized devotedness.

In consuming the Burnt Offering the fire takes up to
God that which is well pleasing to Him. And yet even
in the Burnt Offering there may be the activity of
judgment, for the action of fire is twofold. It consumes that which it cannot purify; it purifies that
which it cannot consume. And so in the Burnt Offering, as well as in the Sin Offering, there is a participation in the moral dispositions of God, an acquiesence in
judgment.

There is therefore a subjective and an objective aspect to the action of the fire.

> "Fire ascending seeks the sun;
> Rivers to the ocean run."

Each seeks its source. And in the realm of the
spiritual the fire which ascends must have first come
from Heaven. The fire for Israel's altar was lit thus at
the consecration of Aaron and his sons. "There came
forth fire from before Jehovah, and consumed upon the
altar the burnt-offering and the fat * *" (Lev. 9:24).
And when the dedication of Solomon's temple took
place "the fire came down from heaven, and consumed
the burnt-offering and the sacrifices" (II Chron. 7:1).
We are not, then, without positive warrant for associat-
ing the action of the fire with Divine qualities and
activities.

It is a part of the limitation of humanity that we
never see things as a whole. In neither the physical or
spiritual realms is it possible for us to do so. Every
material object has more than one side, but no man
ever saw both of the sides simultaneously. We cannot

see anything as an entirety. So also is it in the spiritual sphere. And thus our apprehension of God, and of moral truth, is first on this side and then on that side, but never as a whole. We see justice and we see mercy, but we cannot see them as one quality. We see pity and we see severity, but we cannot see them as one. **But in God they are one.** God's determination to punish sin and His disposition to forgive sin are reconciled in His own nature and constitute one quality. These qualities and dispositions are aspects of love. And so it comes to pass that salvation is accomplished by acts and processes of judgment. Indeed, we might define salvation as that achievement of grace in which it triumphantly confronts the fact of sin and the fact of death, and all that they entail, and accomplishes a deliverance through acts and processes of judgment.

God is One, but we cannot see Him thus.

There is an element in the character of God which expresses itself in utter sacrifice. Its symbol is blood. It is an eternal element. The Lamb was slain before the foundation of the world. And, similarly, there is an element in the character of God which expresses itself in consuming energy. Its symbol is fire. And it is an eternal element. If we apprehend this we may better understand some of the allusions to fire and its everlastingness. "Who among us", says Isaiah, "shall dwell with the devouring fire? who among us shall dwell with everlasting burnings"? He answers his own question. And his answer is this: "he that walketh righteously, and speaketh uprightly; he that despiseth the gain of oppressions, that shaketh his hands from holding of bribes, that stoppeth his ears from hearing of blood, and shutteth his eyes from seeing evil * *". Is not the Prophet describing an intense activity in the Divine nature under the figure of fire? Are not the

solemn warnings which we read in the closing verses
of the 9th chapter of Mark analagous to this?

"If thine eye offend thee, pluck it out: it is better for
thee to enter into the kingdom of God with one eye,
then having two eyes to be cast into (Gehenna, *marg.
A. S. V.*) hell fire: where their worm dieth not, and
the fire is not quenched. For every one shall be salted
with fire, * *".

We have said that fire expresses a spiritual element
in the character of God, and the activity of judgment.
It has also been suggested that this activity is within
the area of redemption, for the passover sacrifice,
which laid the foundation of the redemption, was not
burned. The sacrifices which were consumed were
those that were offered up by a redeemed people, and
their object was to restore and maintain an impaired
fellowship. If this be so, then the judgment symbolized
by the fire is **redeeming judgment**.

In connection with the tabernacle ritual there were
three fires: the fire that consumed those Sin Offerings
that were taken outside the Camp, the fire on the
Altar of Burnt Offering and the fire on the Altar of Incense. The Altar of Burnt Offering occupied a central
place in relation to these fires. It, as it were, bridged
the chasm between an alienated people outside the
Camp and God who was within the veil.

Now we know that the fire on the altar of incense
was taken from the Altar of Burnt Offering, and although there is no direct statement concerning the fire
that consumed the sacrifices outside the Camp, we may
infer that it was from the same source. And this is not
a mere inference, for the Altar of Burnt Offering and
the place of burning outside the Camp were linked together in that the place of burning was the depository
of the ashes which were taken from beneath the Altar

of Burnt Offering *(Lev. 4:12; 6:11)*. And if the fire on the Altar of Burnt Offering was a supernatural fire and, ideally at least, it seems to have been so, then the fire, or fires, kindled from it were this also. It is true that the sons of Aaron were required to put fire upon the altar as a part of the ritual, but the strict requirement that it should never be allowed to go out may carry the inference that ideally it was not natural fire *(Lev. 1:7; 6:13)*. That fire was taken to the Altar of Incense within the veil.

There is no thought of judgment there. The action of the fire brings out from the frankincense that which is altogether delectible. But the Altar of Incense is not detached from the other altars. Not only is the fire brought there from the Altar of Burnt Offering, the blood is brought there from the Sin Offering outside the Camp. Thus man's deepest sinfulness, his innate depravity, his spiritual helplessness is represented at the throne of God, and that in a cloud of perpetual incense before Jehovah. The fire releases the perfume: it is ever thus.

NOTE TO CHAPTER IX.

The question is sometimes raised as to whether the fire spoken of in connection with Divine judgment is literal fire. The form of the question is unsatisfactory. Were it not literal fire it could accomplish nothing. The matter in doubt is rather as to whether the fire is **material** fire. It would seem that in some instances it is so, and in some instances it is not.

The closing words of Isaiah's prophecies and the judgment spoken of in the 25th chapter of Matthew may serve as illustrations of the one and the other. "It shall come to pass", says Isaiah, "that from one new moon to another, and from one Sabbath to another, shall all flesh come to worship before Me, saith Jehovah. And they shall go forth, and look upon the dead bodies of the men that have transgressed against Me: for their worm shall not die, neither shall their fire be quenched; and they shall be an abhorring unto all flesh".

It can hardly be doubted that Isaiah is contemplating millennial conditions, and the setting of the prediction is in the kingdom age. The place to which the peoples are coming with one accord for the worship of Jehovah must be Jerusalem. The place of burning to which the people "go forth" is therefore outside of the sacred city. There could hardly be any doubt as to what the location is. It is a description of the Valley of the Son of Hinnom—the place spoken of in later times as Gehenna. It was a place with a very sordid history. It was there that the kings of Judah had erected heathen altars and burned their children in the fires to heathen gods. Josiah in his zeal polluted it, and it afterward became the cesspool of the city. Isaiah seems to see a revival of this place of pollution in the millennial age, or perhaps on the threshold of that age. Other Prophets describe the judgments which will overtake the nations which oppose the Messiah's rule and resist His authority. Isaiah sees many of these enemies of God as having been put to death, and their bodies cast without burial into these incessantly burning fires. And where the fire does not reach, the worms feed upon the carcases. There would hardly seem to be any doubt that this fire is material fire.

The scene described in the 25th chapter of Matthew appears also to be on the threshold of the millennial age, or at approximately that time. And the judgment portrayed there seems to take place in the same vicinity. The nations of the world are being judged. Those who find themselves upon the King's left hand are sent away into the "age abiding fire, prepared for the devil and his angels." "And these shall go away into age-abiding punishment, but the righteous into age-abiding life." Whether we take this language figuratively or literally the fire could hardly be material fire. The general inference is that it is to have a sustained effect. The nations consigned to it are said to go away into age-abiding punishment (or, as Young translates it: restraint). This would not be the effect of material fire: it would consume. The fire here spoken of seems to be an active agent in an age-abiding punishment, or restraint. There are indeed many questions in connection with it which we cannot answer, but the fire referred to would seem to be spiritual rather than material fire, and there may be a clue to the nature and the effect of this judgment in the history of the Children of Israel in the wilderness. In the 1st verse of the 11th chapter of Numbers we read that the fire of Jehovah burned among the people who complained, and consumed them that were in the uttermost parts of the camp. May it be, therefore, that the nations in question will be removed to remote parts of the earth where they will be under severe discipline, under constant restraint?—where the fire of God will burn among them as it did in remote parts of the camp of Israel.

If the nations here spoken of are the nations living upon the earth at the time of the second advent of Christ, they have not been the subjects of a resurrection, and yet their life appears to be indefinitely prolonged: they are at least spoken of in connection with an age-abiding process. And this process involves the action of fire. Moreover, God anticipated this before the eruption of evil. It was "prepared". It points, therefore, to a provision in His own nature for dealing with evil. But these are mysteries into which we cannot penetrate.

CHAPTER X.

THE BURNT OFFERING

THE opening sentence of the Book of Leviticus defines in general terms the offerings which may be brought acceptably to the altar of burnt offering: they must be of the cattle, of the herd and of the flock. Inasmuch as Meal Offerings and Drink Offerings were a part also of the altar ritual, it may be that it is here assumed, as it is elsewhere expressly implied, that the Meal Offerings and Drink Offerings were adjuncts of the Burnt Offerings. The remainder of the chapter has to do with Burnt Offerings.

The Burnt Offerings were in distinction to the other four classes of offerings enumerated in the first seven chapters of Leviticus. The Burnt Offerings were **all for God**. They were the only class of offerings that were uniformly so.‡

It has already been observed that the altar was regarded as the "table of Jehovah", and we have seen that the Peace Offering was pre-eminently a symbol of fellowship—of communion. But fellowship involves common interests, common participations, common delights. What is it that the heart of God delights to feed upon? Is it not the excellencies of Christ? And when we approach the table of fellowship, that which God offers for our nourishment and satisfaction is Christ. But God could never have done this had not Christ first offered Himself in utter devotion to God, to be the food of His people. And it is that complete devotion which we witness, in symbol, in the Burnt Offering.

---

‡The Sin Offerings were also, in a sense, exclusively for God, when offered for the entire nation, or for the high priest as its representative. No part of them was partaken of by either the priests or the people.

It is suitable, then, that the Burnt Offering should
have been placed first in order, and we are not surprised to find that this offering is basic to all the other
offerings, and that the altar should be designated the
altar of **burnt offering**.

The Burnt Offering was to be of the herd or of the
flock, but pigeons and doves might be alternatively
offered. How unspeakably wonderful is this conde-
scending humility of Christ! The Son of God, the Lord
of Glory, the Creator of the Universe, the One who
formed our bodies and framed our spirits, and holds
us in our life invites us to think of Him as an ox, as a
goat, as a sheep, as a pigeon, as a dove. This is something that we cannot adequately appreciate. Our
moral natures have received such a twist through sin
that it is almost impossible for us to conceive of the
conjunction in one personality of unlimited power and
unmeasured humility. But that is what He is; what
He has.

The second requirement was that the offering must
be a **male without blemish:**—perfection and virility.

The keenest scrutiny of friend and foe has been
turned upon the character of Christ for nineteen centuries, and no one has yet discovered a flaw. Dr.
Horace Bushnell calls attention to the fact that as a
"first peculiarity at the root of His character," He begins life as a perfect youth. No other character in all
literature has ever been painted in this way. But from
His earliest infancy the picture is drawn with these
lines. As a babe He is described as "that holy thing":
as a child He "grew, and waxed strong in spirit, filled
with wisdom, and the grace of God was upon Him".
Was there ever another child described in terms like
these? The offering was to be a "male without blemish".

But the spotless childhood ripened into a blameless manhood. He is the only character in all history who never confesses a sin, never acknowledges a fault, **never repents** or feels the need to repent. It was to be without blemish.

It is next stated that the worshipper must bring the sacrifice, as the margin has it, "that he may be accepted". This language is not used in connection with the Sin Offering. There is suggestion here of the unqualified delight which God takes in it. It is something which is, without reserve, "acceptable" to Him. The Sin Offering was not thus offered. It was taken outside the Camp, as something which God must dismiss from His presence, and was there burned.

The Burnt Offering was, moreover, to be presented "at the door of the tabernacle", and thus "before Jehovah".

In the fourth verse it is said that the offerer shall put his hand upon the head of the Burnt Offering, and it shall be accepted for him, to make atonement for him. But if we would understand the import of the Burnt Offerings we must keep in mind that this was not an atonement for trespass—for wrong doing. It was an atonement for deficiency, for everything lacking in the worshipper which was expressed in the offering. And it would seem that the laying on of the hand symbolized the **dedication** of the sacrifice for that purpose.

But the offerer was not only to present the victim at the door of the tabernacle before Jehovah, and to place his hand upon its head; he must also put it to death. "And he shall kill the bullock before Jehovah". But this is not a Sin Offering, and the slaying of the sacrifice in this type of offering may be intended to express the fullest measure of devotion, "even unto death", rather than an expiation for sin. Yet the idea of expiation is not absent even in the Burnt Offering; it would seem to be expressed, however, rather in the laying on of the hands than in the act of putting the victim to death. The significance of the act of slaying will be observed upon in a subsequent chapter.

It is next stated that "he shall flay the Burnt-offering, and cut it into its pieces" *(A. S. V.)*. (The personal pronoun here would appear to refer to the high priest.) Everything is thus opened and exposed. The skin is torn off, and the inward parts dissected and scrutinized. What man is there who would desire to have every secret thought, every hidden motive, every vagrant imagination opened up to the light in the presence of his fellow men? But as we pass on to the ninth verse we see that the type is necessarily imperfect and inadequate. "But its inwards and its legs shall he wash with water" *(A. S. V.)*. The sacrifice was not clean. It must needs be washed in water to express the purity of Christ.

There were several alternatives permitted in the selection of the victims for the Burnt Offerings. The sacrifice might be an ox *(vs. 3)*, or a goat or a sheep *(vs. 10)*, or a dove or pigeon *(vs. 14)*. There would seem to be a twofold intention in this. We have on the one hand **aspects** of the character of Christ, but, on the other hand we have the varied **apprehensions** of the believer. The thought of the varied apprehensions of the believer may be noticed in connection with other offerings. We notice more particularly here that in these alternatives we have aspects of Christ.

What are the oustanding ideas?

The OX is the symbol of patient endurance, of unremitting toil. The SHEEP suggests unresisting submission. The GOAT is associated typically with sin. The DOVE expresses harmlessness.

Of the four narratives of the earthly life of Christ, one is devoted to presenting Him as the patient, unwearied toiler, the Servant of Jehovah, always at work. The record of Mark seems to be symbolized by the ox.

The sheep, Isaiah reminds us, was **shorn** *(Is. 53:7)*. It submitted to the process without murmur. So also with Christ. He gave up His home; He gave up His leisure; He gave up His reputation, and, finally, they took from Him even His garments, so that the same Prophet graphically says: He was cut off and had nothing.

The goat was the animal sacrificed on the annual Day of Atonement, and can hardly be disassociated from the thought of sin. And although the Burnt Offering was not a sin offering, yet the central element of the devotion of Christ as a burnt offering was His readiness to be "made sin".

The disciples were admonished to be as harmless as doves.

But what is the spiritual significance for us of the daily burnt offering? In what does the Burnt Offering avail for us? If it be not a "Sin Offering", in what does it help us as sinners?

(a) It gives the essential value to the Sin Offering. This is repeatedly expressed in the ritual. The Sin Offerings were required to be killed "in the place where the Burnt Offering" was killed. The one was fundamental to the other *(Lev. 6:25)*. But not only so; the carcase of the Sin Offering when taken without the Camp must be burned on the ashes of the Burnt Offering. This is seen by a comparison of Leviticus 4: 12 and Leviticus 6: 11.

(b) It atones for everything in us which is not what

the Burnt Offering was: complete devotion to God. We need more than the forgiveness of trespasses; we need more than an atonement for our innate sinfulness. There is a positive life of consecration to the will of God. And even that aspect of the life of Christ was vicarious. And as a vicarious sacrifice it did more than lay the foundation for the Sin Offering; it is made over to us as an element of the merit of Christ. It was moreover a **daily** sacrifice, and we need daily to plead the burnt offering aspect of the death of Christ. And with every Burnt Offering there was, day by day, a Meal Offering. The meaning of this we will see in the following chapter.

NOTE TO CHAPTER X.

The New Testament gives us seven objectives for the death of Christ, but not one of these objectives expresses the Burnt Offering aspect of His death.

He died for the ungodly *(Rom. 5:6)*.

He died for our sins *(I Cor. 15:3)*.

He died to bring us to God *(I Peter 3:18)*.

He died that He might deliver us from this present evil world *(Gal. 1:4)*.

He died that they which live should not henceforth live unto themselves, but unto Him who died for them and rose again *(II Cor. 5:15)*.

He died for us that whether we wake or sleep, we should live together with Him *(I Thess. 5:10)*.

He died that He might be Lord both of the dead and living *(Rom. 14:9)*.

Each of these are expressly stated as objectives for the death of Christ, but it is in the words which the Psalmist puts into the mouth of Christ as He comes into the world, that there is given us the Burnt Offering aspect of His death:

> "Sacrifice and offering Thou didst not desire; mine ears hast Thou opened: burnt offering and sin offering hast Thou not required. Then said I, Lo, I come: in the volume of the Book it is written of Me, I delight to do Thy will, O My God; yea, Thy Law is within My heart" *(Ps. 40:6-8)*.

That is the Burnt Offering. And in the Garden of Gethsemane, in that agony of soul which was "even unto death", He, as it were, lays His hand upon the sacrifice, as in the perfect submission of His will He offers Himself as a living oblation to God. "Not My will, but Thine, be done".

CHAPTER XI.

THE MEAL OFFERING

IN the first chapter of the Book of Leviticus there is
given the ritual of the Burnt Offering. This offering stands at the beginning because fundamentally it is
the most essential, the most important one. Will you
recall its characteristics? It was to be of the herd or
of the flock; it was a **living** sacrifice. It was a male,
and thus the symbol of virility and strength. It was
without blemish; there must be no fault. It was offered "for acceptance"; it was a sacrifice in which
God could take unqualified delight as representing the
full and perfect devotion of Christ. The blood was to
be sprinkled upon the altar, for the blood was the
symbol of the life of the victim. It was to be cut into
its pieces, and the inward parts were to be washed with
water; the whole was to be exposed and opened up;
but inasmuch as there was not inward purity in the
victim it must be cleansed to express the purity of
Christ. And, finally, it was to be all burned; it was all
for God. And the ashes being, as it would seem, the
symbol of death were to be taken away to a clean place
outside the Camp,—to a clean place, for they were
sacred ashes; outside the Camp, for they expressed
the essence of death.

The Burnt Offering, then, gives us the Godward aspect of the atoning work of Christ and that is the fundamental aspect. The first concern of Christ in coming
into the world was to do the will of God; in doing that
He met the needs of men.

As we consider these sacrifices we are contemplating
Christ: they are symbolic pictures written beforehand
of the incarnate One. They show us His person, His
character and His work from this point of view and

from that. What then was it that He offered to God in
the Burnt Offering?   In that offering He fulfilled His
complete duty to God as **man**.   And in so doing He had
nothing left over for us; He needed that complete, that
entire obedience for Himself as a man.   It was the devotion that God required.   Nevertheless we participate
in it, for He identifies Himself with us, and us with
Himself.

The Burnt Offering was, in all this, a "sweet savour"
offering.

Now, what was the Meal Offering?   It also was a
sweet savor offering but it was a very different **kind**
of sweet savor offering from the Burnt Offering.   It
was not a living sacrifice; there was no blood.   It was
of the products of the earth.   It was corn, or that whic'
comes from corn, flour: it was flour, or that which is
produced from flour, bread and cakes.   And it was not
consumed on the altar, except the "memorial": it was
eaten by the priests.

But notice that it was **processed** corn and **processed**
flour.   If the offering were of corn it must be beaten
and dried by the fire *(Lev. 2:14)*.   If it were flour it
was processed corn in the nature of things, but it was
also to be **fine** flour.

And, then, in addition, there was to be oil, salt and
frankincense, but **no** leaven and **no** honey.

In the Meal Offering, then, we would seem to have
Christ fulfilling His duty to **man**.   It is not specifically
Christ fulfilling His duty to the sinner, or meeting the
needs of the sinner, **as such**,—the Sin Offering expresses that, but as a man on the earth giving Himself for
the nourishment of man.   But even this has a Godward aspect; a "memorial" was consumed upon the
altar.

If this be so, for what do these symbols stand?

First of all, it was processed corn and processed flour, that is: it was not the bare products of the earth, even though it might be a perfect product. It is difficult for us to understand how a sinless man could need the **discipline** of life for His perfection. And yet that was so. "Though He were a Son, yet learned He obedience by the things which He suffered". He was made "perfect through sufferings". He needed the grinding and the sifting and the bruising, and the heat of the fire. And if He did, how much more do we?

And it was **fine** flour. There were no unevennesses. This would have made Him unique if nothing else had. He is the only "even" Man the world has ever seen. Even as a child there were no unevennesses in His disposition or character. He was advanced but not forward; marvelous but not precocious; conscious of an individual responsibility to God but never unmindful of the natural obligations to parental authority. And as a Man, what perfect balance and proportion in all those things that made up the texture of His full orbed personality!

There was not in Him, in the way in which we find it in other men, some characteristic predominating conspicuously. Other men are daring or conservative or cowardly: they are practical or artistic or philosophical: they have an aptitude for detail or a genius for engineering great enterprises: they have a faculty for accomplishing things by personal contact or they have the power to move the emotions of large masses of men. But in Christ we find every component of human perfection, both as to endowment and character. He had no strong or weak points. It was FINE flour. In Him there was a perfect blending and balance of every virtue and attribute: compassion, meekness,

courage, patience, zeal, anger, tenderness, scorn, pity,
—a holy hatred and a Divine love. It was **fine** flour.

But will you notice that there were a number of
grades of this processed corn or processed flour,—this
Meal Offering. It might be fine flour or unleavened
cakes baken in an oven, or cakes baken in a pan, or
cakes baken in a frying pan, or ears of corn beaten
and dried.

Why this diversity, these alternatives? In the first
place, to meet the varying abilities of the worshippers.
The well-to-do might be able to bring fine flour in a
silver charger; those in comfortable circumstances
would possess an oven; those less well off would have
the pan, or fire plate, and the very poor would have no
utensil but a frying pan. But God accommodates Himself to whatever may be the ability of the offerer. He
never requires that which we do not possess.

But when we look at these grades of the Meal Offering symbolically we see the varying apprehensions of
Christ with which the worshipper approaches God.
The spiritual apprehensions may be very meager; the
offerer may, so to speak, have the most poverty-strick-
en apprehension of Christ, but if it is **Christ** that he
brings to God, God will receive him, even though his
apprehension of Christ be only, as it were, a pancake.

But notice further: the Meal Offering was anointed
or mingled with oil. The anointing seems to denote
separation or setting apart *(Gen. 28:18)*. And inasmuch as the Spirit does this, the oil may be a symbol
of the Holy Spirit. But it seems also to denote a **quality**,—the quality of joy, or a spiritual state which is
in keeping with consecration. The Psalmist says that
oil is given to man "to make his face to shine"; Isaiah
speaks of the "oil of joy for mourning"; of the Messiah
it is said that God has anointed Him with "the oil of

gladness". There is in each of these references the conception of gladness and joy. But in **anointing** with oil there is the thought of separation to a vocation, and Isaiah causes the Messiah to declare that Jehovah "anointed" Him for His ministry among men, and Peter declares that God anointed Him "with the Holy Spirit and with power", and that He "went about doing good, and healing all that were oppressed of the devil". **That** was the **Meal** Offering.

And then there was salt. Salt preserves from corruption. Accordingly to this day, among the most diverse peoples, salt is the recognized symbol of incorruption and unchanging perpetuity. Among the Arabs of to-day, for example, when a compact or covenant is made between parties it is the custom that each eat of salt, which is passed around on the blade of a sword; by which act they regard themselves as bound to be true, each to the other, even at the peril of life. In like manner, in India and other eastern countries, the usual word for perfidy and breach of faith is literally, "unfaithfulness to the salt," and a man will say: "Can you mistrust me; have I not eaten your salt?" Salt preserves from corruption, and that is what a godly life should do; it should preserve from corruption the society in which it moves.

And, finally, there was frankincense. That was fragrance. It is not the **actions** that make the life fragrant; it is the quality and spirit of the life. There was an aroma about the life of Christ that ascended up to God as sweet incense. **That** was not for man; the frankincense was all burnt upon the altar; it was all for God.

But there was to be no leaven, for leaven is the symbol of corruption. And there was to be no honey, for honey is natural sweetness, and it sours under the action of fire.

These, then, were the ingredients and those things that were expressly excluded from the composition of the Meal Offering.

But notice that "he", that is the offerer, "shall pour oil upon it, and put frankincense thereon". And again: "and every oblation of thy Meal-Offering shalt thou season with salt" (A. S. V.). These are the accompaniments which are designed to make the oblation pleasing to God; they are the symbols of that which is spiritually delectable. And the **offerer** puts them on the oblation. In this he, as it were, acknowledges a standard of requirement which must be met to render him acceptable. It is a perfect standard. The life has been lived. But the ideal has not been put before us to dismay us. It is **for** us. **Every priest may partake**, and "he that eateth Me, even he shall live by Me".

Every **priest** may partake. This, like the Burnt Offering is a sacrifice in which the sinner, as such, has no part. It was on this account that should the priest offer a meal offering for **himself** it was to be wholly burnt (Lev. 6:22, 23). But the Meal Offering is not exclusively for God; man has a part in it. And the priest is the worshipper idealized. As such he partakes. But the sinner, as such, does not find his satisfaction or his nourishment in the perfect fulfillment of Christ's duty as a man among men. But God and the priest partake together.

And observe, it is **his** handful which the priest puts on the altar. It is thus an "offering" which man brings to God, and which God accepts.

But notice further that this handful is a "memorial". The earthly life of Christ has passed into history; it is a sacred memory: it can never repeat itself, but it will forever be a "memorial" before God.

NOTE TO CHAPTER XI.

Will you notice the relation of the Meal Offering to the Burnt Offering, for this is very important. You observe that the Burnt Offering is first in order, and the Burnt Offering was a continual offering; morning and night a perpetual burnt offering was upon the altar, for the people as a whole. But the Meal Offering was subordinate to the Burnt Offering. This is seen in the directions given for the offerings at the annual feasts. Over and over again the Burnt Offering is spoken of, and then following, the Meal Offering is alluded to as "its Meal Offering", or "the Meal Offering thereof" (See Numbers 29). What does this teach? If the Burnt Offering speaks of man's duty to God and the Meal Offering of man's duty to man, it reminds us that whilst God does not belittle or disparage man's duty to man, the discharge of that alone does not constitute an acceptable oblation. It is secondary and subordinate. And in the deepest and fullest sense man does not ever fulfil that duty. You remember that Cain brought the Meal Offering, and he was a **murderer**! But Christ **did** fully meet all the requirements of the Meal Offering; He discharged His full duty to man as man. Nevertheless, there was more required of Him than that: He must bring the Burnt Offering as well. And His Meal Offering was an adjunct to the Burnt Offering.

CHAPTER XII.

THE PEACE OFFERING

THE sacrificial system of the Old Testament centered around the tabernacle. But so soon as
we say that, there arise in the mind one question after
another which only revelation can answer,—to which
only the Scriptures can furnish a reply.

Why was there a tabernacle?

Why was there a sacrificial system?

Why were not sacrifices acceptable anywhere?

You will recall that sacrifices **had** been permitted
and accepted without regard to an appointed place.
And yet, perhaps by the law of association, even the
patriarchs seemed to feel a special fitness in certain
places for the offering up of sacrifices to God. But
when the law was given there were restrictions imposed. And in the wilderness the tabernacle became
the meeting place between Jehovah and Israel.

There was thus impressed upon the Nation, and
through them upon mankind, that access to God was
not a natural approach, that sin had caused a disloca-
tion, and had erected a barrier which could only be
bridged by obedience to God. And that was not by
man's obedience, but by that obedience enveloped,
as it were, by the obedience of Another. Man must
come in God's way, and that was by means of the
Altar, the Sacrifice and the Priest. And the priest
offered the sacrifice upon the altar at the door of the
tabernacle. And thus the altar, sacrifice, priest and
tabernacle constituted together a group of related
symbols and types which were full of spiritual meanings, and which told out the truths of redemption in
parabolic form.

The altar was the table of Jehovah (*Ezek. 44:16;*

41:22; Mal. 1:7,12). That is particularly suggestive in connection with the Peace Offering, as we shall see, for it expresses the fact that God is seeking, through the sacrificial ritual and that for which it stands, a recovery of fellowship with man.

This idea of the table spread runs all through the Scriptures. When God made a covenant with the Children of Israel at Mount Sinai we are told that Moses and Aaron, Nadab and Abihu, and seventy of the elders of Israel, went up into the mount, and they saw the God of Israel, * * * * and **did eat and drink** *(Exod. 24:9-11).* On a previous occasion, when Jethro was visiting Moses, we are told that he took a burnt offering and sacrifices for God, and Aaron came and all the elders of Israel **to eat bread with Moses' father-in-law before God** *(Exod. 18:12).* When God prescribed religious convocations for the Nation, those convocations were termed "Feasts" *(Lev. 23).* When, subsequently, the laws of tithing were promulgated the tithes were to be **eaten before the Lord** *(Deut. 12:17,18 and 14:22-26 and 28,29).* And the last hours which Jesus spent with the disciples before His death were in sacred fellowship around the social board, and He perpetuated that fellowship for the generations to come. And one of the last events depicted in the Scriptures is that of a holy meal yet to be celebrated, —the marriage supper of the Lamb. And in setting up the tabernacle God pitched a tent among men, to which He could invite them to come and feast with Him.

There were, as we have seen, five different forms of offering or oblation prescribed for the tabernacle ritual. And each of these had its particular meaning as exhibiting some aspect of the person, character and work of Christ.

In the burnt sacrifice we have Christ as Man, exhibiting His full devotion to **God**. In the meal offering we have Christ as Man, exhibiting His full devotion to **man**. These two are basic. Without that which they symbolize Christ could never have been man's Redeemer.

The Peace Offering is central. It stands in between the Burnt Offering and the Meal Offering on the one hand, and the Sin Offering and the Trespass Offering on the other. In the Burnt Offering. and the Meal Offering we see God in Christ approaching man; in the Sin Offering and the Trespass Offering we see man in Christ approaching God. In the Peace Offering we have the meeting together of these five offerings and the resulting communion.

The ritual of the Peace Offering was much fuller and more elaborate than that of the other offerings, and in it we have both the Burnt Offering and the Meal Offering. In Leviticus 3:3-5 we have the living sacrifice and the consumption upon the altar,—a modified form of the Burnt Offering: in Leviticus 7:12-14 we have as an accompaniment of the Peace Offering, a Meal Offering. This Meal Offering was enjoined when the Peace Offering was a "thanksgiving". It is very significant, moreover, that in this Meal Offering, which accompanied the Peace Offering, some of the cakes might be, nay, were required to be, of leavened bread. And furthermore, that one of the leavened cakes, as well as of the unleavened, was to be presented as a heave offering to Jehovah, before being partaken of by the priests (See Lev. 7:14). God recognizes that human praise will be imperfect, and will be mixed with sin.

The Meal Offering, then, was not exclusively a type of Christ. It was the one offering that was also a type of the Congregation. This is seen again in the Meal Offering which was presented on the Day of Pentecost, —two loaves baken with leaven *(Lev. 23:17)*. But if you will look back to Verse 13 of that same chapter you will see that no leaven is mentioned there, for **that** Meal Offering was a type of Christ.

But notice again: it was the Peace Offering presented as a **thanksgiving** of which the Meal Offering was a **stipulated** part. Praise which ignores man's duty to man is a superficial mockery.

But observe once more: the Peace Offering of thanksgiving was to be eaten the same day *(Lev. 7: 15)*. Praise is not to be stale; we are not to delay to give thanks *(Lev. 19:6-8)*.

But observe again: the portion of the Peace Offering which was to be burned upon the altar, or to be waved for a wave offering, must be brought with the offerer's own hands *(Lev. 7:28, 29)*. God cannot either enter into fellowship, or accept praise, by proxy.

The central conception, then, of the Peace Offering, as distinguished from the other offerings, was that it distinctively symbolizes **communion**. It was shared in by Jehovah, by those who waited upon the altar and by the worshipper. There was a portion for GOD, a portion for the PRIESTS and a portion for the OF-FERER *(Lev. 3:9-11; 7:14 and 32-34; 7:15-18)*.

The priests occupied an intermediary position between the people and God. They not only measured the distance between man and God, they, so to speak, idealized the existing relationship and the resulting fellowship. The portions of the Peace Offerings assigned to the priests were therefore choice portions expressive of vigor and affection,—the right shoulder and the breast. All the remainder of the Peace Offerings, save the fat, which was Jehovah's portion, was consumed by the offerers.

Now we see an additional reason why the sacrifices must be offered at an appointed place, which was God's house. The altar is the table of Jehovah; He is feasting. He is feasting with man. In the Peace Offering God and man are reconciled, and as reconciled they meet together to rejoice in, and feast upon, the excellencies of Christ.

A casual reference has already been made, in a previous chapter, to the groupings of the five offerings in the first seven chapters of the Book of Leviticus as to the change in the order in the second grouping. The extended sections in which the sacrifices are described in detail present them in an order which places the Peace Offering in the center of the group: the more condensed sections which follow, and which give the Law of the Offerings, place the Peace Offering last. Both arrangements have their significance. The Peace Offering is central when we are considering man's· restoration to God. On the one side we have in the Burnt Offering and the Meal Offering God approaching man; on the other side in the Trespass and the Sin Offering man approaching God. In the Peace Offering in the center we have the resulting communion. But in the alternative arrangement it is as a **consummation** that the Peace Offering is placed as the last in order of the five. It is this consummation for which God waits; for which Christ died; for which creation groans; for which the church prays,—the day of a restored communion between earth and heaven, between man and God.

"And the work of righteousness shall be peace; and the effect of righteousness quietness and assurance for ever" (*Is. 32:17*).

CHAPTER XIII.

THE SIN OFFERING

THERE is something brought out in the ritual of the Sin Offering which is not seen in connection with any other of the sacrifices, and that is the **persons** of the **offerers** and their relative standing and responsibilities. There are in the 4th chapter of the Book of Leviticus separate sections devoted to the offering of the Sin Offering by "the priest that is anointed", (vs. 3); "the whole congregation", (vs. 13); "a ruler", (vs. 22); "any one of the common people", (vs. 27). The victim required, and the ritual prescribed, were identical for the anointed priest and for the entire congregation, for the high priest represented in his person the Nation as such. In respect to both of these the sacrifice required was a bullock. It was, moreover, only in the instance of the offering being for the entire congregation, or for the high priest, that blood from the sacrifice was taken into the Holy Place, and sprinkled before the veil, and put upon the horns of the altar of incense. The reason for taking the blood into the presence of God in these cases was undoubtedly because God was in covenant relation with the Nation, whereas the covenant was not with individual Israelites.

But why are the persons of the offerers before us in the Sin Offering? The Sin Offering, and the Trespass Offering, give us the manward side of the approach; in them we see man in Christ approaching God. And it is man as a sinner that is making the approach, and he is presenting sin offerings and guilt offerings. But guilt is measured by responsibility, and responsibility by privilege. There is a greater weight of responsibility resting upon the Nation than upon a ruler, and upon a ruler than upon one of the common people. This varying measure of responsibility is expressed in the grades of the offerings presented, but in the Sin Offering, as in the other offerings, the grades also symbolize the apprehension of the worshipper. The greater the spiritual privilege the clearer should be the apprehension of Christ as the offering for sin: that is why the persons of the offerers, as representing privilege and responsibility, and the grades, as representing individual apprehension, are so closely related.

As we said in the previous chapter, in the Burnt Offering and the Meal Offering we see God in Christ approaching man: in the Sin Offering and the Trespass Offering we see man in Christ approaching God. And in approaching God man is both consciously and unconsciously sinful. He is conscious of having committed trespasses; that is expressed in the Trespass Offering. But there is something deeper than that, and of which he may not become at once aware. There are things which are "hidden from him". Notice the reiteration of this in the text. "If it be hidden from him" (Lev. 5:2); "And it be hid from him" (Lev. 5:3 and 4).

Man is not aware of sin in its deepest sense until God makes him aware of it thus. He is ignorant of it (Lev. 4:1, 13, 22, 27). The Sin Offering makes provision for a man who has sinned and does not know it. But he is made aware of it. And so we read: "when he knoweth of it, then he shall be guilty * *, when he shall be guilty in one of these things, that he shall confess that he hath sinned" (Lev. 5:4, 5).

We are not judged by human standards of what constitutes sin,—not by man's standards, but by

God's. If man's standards were the criterion of sin and righteousness the moral universe would rest upon a precarious and shifting foundation indeed. But the standard is God's, and because that is so, man must be made aware of sin. And it is when he has been thus made aware that he presents the Sin Offering. And it is, moreover, a disclosure to his conscience and heart of what the Burnt Offering and the Meal Offering signify, of utter devotion to God and full duty to man, that awakens and deepens in him a sense of the imperative need of the Sin Offering. He increasingly realizes, not only what he has **done** or **not done**, but what he **is** and what he **is not**.

But there is a provision made in the Sin Offering for very meager apprehensions of the sacrificial work of Christ, as an offering for sin. In the 5th chapter of Leviticus, where shortcoming or defilement is in view rather than the person of the offerer, we read that if he be unable to bring a lamb (*vs. 7*), he shall bring two turtle doves or two young pigeons. But if he be not able to bring even these (*vs. 11*) he may bring fine flour for his sin offering. God does not accept men on the basis of their apprehensions of the atoning work of Christ. Their apprehensions may be very meager and poverty-stricken, they may be deeply deficient, but God looks to see if He can discern faith and whether it be **Christ** that the offerer brings. But notice that these alternative offerings were only to be accepted in the event that the offerer were **unable** to bring a living sacrifice, or the more suitable one prescribed. It was not a question of a worshipper setting up his own standards and introducing his own ideas of what should constitute the basis of reconciliation with God: it is, on the other hand, God coming out and meeting man **where he is**.

In the 4th chapter of Leviticus it is stated that the Sin Offerings are to be brought if those who are concerned have sinned "through ignorance against any of the commandments of the Lord". In the opening part of the 5th chapter we have illustrations of moral weakness or delinquency, as well as of ceremonial impurity, constituting occasions for presenting Sin Offerings. In the four specific cases cited two may be unquestionably classified as sins of ignorance; one of them is certainly not so, but may imply a constitutional weakness expressing itself in moral cowardice; the last one occupies a middle ground as to self-consciousness *(Lev. 5:1-5)*.

The illustration in the first verse is not so much of unconscious sin as of moral infirmity, or momentary weakness, of yielding to the temptation to fail to perform a duty because the performance required moral courage. The scene is in a Court of Law. A witness is on the stand; he has "heard the voice of adjuration," or, as we would say, he has "been sworn." He is under oath; he is to declare as a witness what he has seen or heard concerning the matter at issue. The life, or the punishment, of a friend may be in the balance. He fails to bear his testimony to the facts of which he is cognizant. His silence, whilst it may defeat the ends of justice, may shield a friend. He is overcome because of inherent moral weakness; he holds something back; he does not tell the whole truth. This is not trespass; it is sin. The illustration, however, does not express sin in its deepest sense; it is not a sin of "ignorance". It is shortcoming. And whilst it is hidden from other men, it is not hidden from the man himself. This is one phase of sin; others are expressed in the citations following.

The next illustration takes us to the field. The man

in question has done nothing consciously; he has inadvertently contacted that which is unclean. Certain forms of life had been so designated by the Mosaic Law, and he had unwittingly touched the dead body of such a creature. It is purely ceremonial pollution, but it calls for ceremonial cleansing. The inadvertent unconsciousness of the act; the, so to speak, helplessness of the man, are intended to express the nature of sin. Man is involved in it without his choice before he participates in it by consent: he does not have to do anything to become a sinner: the disclosure must be made to him that he **is** one but it is not the disclosure that constitutes him a sinner: the fact preceded the recognition of it *(Comp. Lev. 5:2 and 3)*.

The third illustration is similar to the second one: it is another form of ceremonial uncleanness, some "uncleanness of man". But the expression used in relation to guilt is different. In the former case it says that if it be hidden from him he shall be guilty; in this case it states: "when he knoweth of it, then he shall be guilty". There is an incipient guilt in respect to sin in the nature, a guilt waiting to be awakened, and there is an aroused guilt. But so long as "it be hidden" from the man, he who is defiled will not bring an offering.

But sometimes the sinful nature will express itself in a self reliance which is outspoken and uncontrolled. "If any one swear rashly with his lips to do evil, or to do good, whatsoever it be that a man shall utter rashly with an oath, and it be hid from him; when he knoweth of it, then he shall be guilty * *" *(A. S. V.)*.

You notice that these four citations are in pairs. The central two are almost identical and concern ceremonial pollution. The two outer ones are in contrast the one to the other. In the first one the man has sworn to express himself, but through a hesitant weakness or cowardice he remains silent. In the last one the man in question is vociferous. He is swearing as to what he will do, or will not do, without even registering in his own mind what he is promising or boasting to effect. Each of these is intended to suggest the working of sin in the nature. In two of them there is entire unconsciousness of the condition; in one of them there might seem to be a form of self-hypnotism; in one only, the first, is the man at once aware of that which is the occasion for the Sin Offering.

In the last analysis we see man in connection with the Sin Offering as the victim of what he **is**, and as the slave of his environment. In one instance of the four specific cases cited he is too fearful to speak; he withholds that which he should express: in another instance he is too self-confident to burden his memory with covenant vows; he speaks that which he should withhold. In the other cases his environment involves him in pollutions of which he was altogether unaware.

Thus, in picture language, God draws the outlines of what we are, of inherent depravity. And that is why we need a Sin Offering.

NOTE TO CHAPTER XIII.

The 5th chapter of Leviticus forms, as we said in a previous chapter, a kind of bridge between the section following it and the one going before. It deals, for the most part, with sins of ignorance but they are sometimes, nevertheless, sins involving **trespasses.** There is thus the occasion for a fusing together of the Sin Offering and the Trespass Offering, and that is

what we see in this chapter. Indeed so marked is this
fusing that although we are still in the Sin Offering
section, yet the offering prescribed is spoken of as a
trespass or guilt offering, and also as a sin offering in
one and the same verse *(Lev. 5:6)*. The sacrifice is
that prescribed for a Sin Offering, but the alternative
phrasing suggests the cloudiness of apprehension upon the part of man as to those distinctions which are
inherent in the words trespass and sin. Whilst God
may see the delinquency as sin, to man it may be but
a trespass, and the offering cannot express more than
he discerns.

As the chapter draws to a close there is an advance
in thought in the direction of emphasizing the trespass aspect and the relative guilt. This is done (a)
by bringing into specific mention trespass in "the holy
things of Jehovah" *(A. S. V.)*, (b) by a higher grade of
offering and (c) by restitution for the wrong, with an
addition of the fifth part thereto. And, then, in the
closing paragraph, we have a widening out, a fusion
and an emphasis which bring us to the threshold of the
Trespass Offering section.

"And if any one sin" *(vs. 17, A. S. V.)* "and do any
of the things which Jehovah hath commanded not to
be done" *(A. S. V.)*. This is specific **trespass**. But
the passage continues: "though he knew it not," and
this is a sin of **ignorance**, which is the prominent
idea of the **Sin** Offering. However, the sacrifice to be
brought is a "ram without blemish" and this is the
trespass offering for one of the common people.

That there is an intended **advance** in thought in the
chapter is evidenced by a comparison of the grades
of the offerings designated in the opening and closing
sections. In verse 6 the sacrifice required is a female
from the flock, a lamb or a kid of the goats. This is

specifically the **Sin** Offering *(see chap. 4, vss. 28 and 32)*. In verse **15** the sacrifice required is a ram without blemish. This is specifically the **Trespass** Offering *(see chap. 6:6)*. We notice, moreover, that the Trespass Offering is of a higher grade than the Sin Offering, for although sin is more penetrating in its nature and more particularly against God, yet the **guilt** is greater in respect to trespass, unless there be a high degree of enlightenment, and this is not pre-supposed as to one of the common people. However, when the entire congregation, or a ruler, were in-volved, the grade of sacrifice for a Sin Offering was correspondingly higher, for there was a higher degree of responsibility *(see chap. 4:14 and 23)*.

CHAPTER XIV.

THE TRESPASS OFFERING

THE Trespass Offering is the last in order of the five offerings prescribed under the Law. It was akin to the Sin Offering and yet distinct from it. The difference between the Sin Offering and the Trespass Offering appears to be that which the two words indicate. Sin is missing the mark; it is coming short. Trespass is passing over it; it is going beyond. In sin there is spiritual deficiency or helplessness; in trespass there is a voluntary and overt act.

All Sin Offerings were for sins of ignorance, of failure, of inadvertence or of helplessness. Usually they were for acts or conditions of which the man was not aware at the time. They were for things which were "hid from him". The spiritual nature of sin could not be expressed through an ordinance more appropriately. Sin is a state; it is because man is in a state of sin that he expresses sin through his personality and his actions, without being aware of it. But when he invades the rights of another, that is trespass.

We have already seen how that in the 5th chapter of Leviticus there is a fusion of the ideas of trespass and sin. The section is indeed the Sin Offering section, and the sacrifices brought are those prescribed for Sin Offerings, until we reach the closing portion of the chapter, and yet they are spoken of as "trespass" or "guilt" offerings. That closing portion is distinctive; it is marked off as a separate section by the commencing words: "And Jehovah spake unto Moses, saying" (*vs. 14, A. S. V.*). It has to do with trespass "in the holy things of Jehovah", and the offering required was the **trespass** or "guilt" offering. Nevcrtheless it is a class of trespasses which are committed "in ignorance" *(see vss. 15, 17, 18, A. S. V.).* And the element of ignorance is a characteristic identified with the **Sin** Offering.

It is not until we reach the 6th chapter that we have the distinctively Trespass Offering section. It is much briefer than any other. It occupies only seven verses, and it has to do exclusively with trespasses between man and man. Yet even such trespasses are against Jehovah *(vs. 2).* But there is nothing said here concerning "ignorance". Man's spiritual condition is such that he is often **ignorant** of his duty to **God**, when he is **aware** of his duty to **man**.

In verses 2 and 3 there are given some illustrations of trespass between man and man. These trespasses have to do almost entirely, perhaps exclusively, with property rights. The only exception might be in that which is described as a "fellowship", or literally: "putting of the hands"; and we may suppose that mutual agreements in such a primitive society would almost certainly concern property.

The expressions which are employed are remarkably comprehensive as to the acquisition of property. There are five classifications: "that which was delivered him to keep", that is a pledge; "or in fellowship", that is as to property held in common or acquired by mutual agreement; "or in a thing taken away by violence", that is stolen property; "or hath deceived his neighbour", that is as to property acquired by sharp practice; "or * * that which was lost", that is property found.

But the emphasis is notably upon the state of heart that occasions the trespass. The prominent ideas throughout are those of lying and deceit and swearing falsely concerning it. The two verses read thus:

"If any one sin, and commit a trespass against the
Lord, and lie unto his neighbour in that which was
delivered him to keep, or in fellowship, or in a thing
taken away by violence, or hath deceived his neighbour; or have found that which was lost, and lieth concerning it, and sweareth falsely; in any of all these that
a man doeth, sinning therein":

Trespass is traced back to a disposition by what
precedes or what follows it. Man tries to cover by
deceit that which he perpetrated by violence or fraud.
Or, on the other hand, he may deceive his neighbor
in order to the subsequent accomplishment of some
sinful design. Trespass is thus linked up with sin.

But you observe that something intervenes before
the presentation of a Trespass Offering. The trespasser must restore "that which he took violently
away, or the thing which he hath deceitfully gotten,
or that which was delivered him to keep, or the lost
thing which he found, or all that about which he
hath sworn falsely"; he must make good the injury.
Restitution must take place before there can be participation in that aspect of Christ's work which is represented by the Trespass Offering.

"Therefore, if thou bring thy gift to the altar, and
there rememberest that thy brother hath ought against
thee; leave there thy gift before the altar, and go thy
way; first be reconciled to thy brother, and then come
and offer thy gift" (Matt. 5:23, 24).

Yes, but there is more than that: he shall add a
fifth part more thereto. This provision appeared in
the previous section in connection with trespass in
the "holy things of Jehovah" (A. S. V.). Observe,
however, in connection with the holy things of Jehovah
that the measure of restitution, to which the fifth part
was to be added, was to be appraised, not by the esti-

mation of the offerer but by the estimation of Moses, and after the shekel of the sanctuary. Our spiritual preceptions are not equal to a true estimation of trespass in holy things.

What is the meaning of adding the fifth part? There are some who think that the first mention of anything in the Scriptures determines the spiritual significance. It would seem as if that might be the case in this instance.

We read in the Book of Genesis of a great famine which affected the whole world. But in Egypt there had been seven years of plenty before the famine began. And the storehouses of Pharaoh had been filled. And when the years of famine came, in process of time the people began to be in want. And they came to Joseph to buy corn. They brought money, but their money became exhausted. They brought their cattle, but their cattle became exhausted. And then they came to Joseph and they confessed that they were in Pharaoh's hands: they were at his mercy. They said:

"We will not hide it from my lord, how that our money is spent; my lord also hath our herds of cattle; thère is not ought left in the sight of my lord but our bodies and our lands: * *   * * buy us and our land for bread".

And so Joseph bought the land and gave them seed to sow, and he said:

"It shall come to pass at the ingatherings, that ye shall give a fifth [part] unto Pharaoh" (A. S. V.).

What did the fifth part mean? that **rent**, for that was what it was: what did it mean? It meant that the land belonged to Pharaoh. It meant that they had lost all right to everything. And similarly when the fifth part was brought with the restitution it meant not only that it was not a **gift** that was being brought, that the restitution was something that was **due**; it signified, if the analogy holds, that the trespasser had put himself and all that he had under tribute to the one to whom he was making amends. The subjects of Pharaoh had lost all their rights; they confessed that they were at his mercy. That is the spirit of the Trespass Offering.

Of course there was a practical consideration, an element of justice behind the requirement. The injured one might have suffered from the trespass beyond its exact equivalent; and the adding of the fifth part was to cover this.

But further than this: the fifth was also two tithes, two-tenths. Was there not here also the thought that in adding the fifth the offerer was satisfying a double responsibility,—to God and man?

But how does responsibility of God arise in connection with trespasses which are exclusively between man and man? There may be a truth concealed in this requirement of the addition of a fifth part which will excite our wonder, if not our incredulity. We have suggested that the two tenths were one for God and one for man. If this be so, then the one for man satisfies the requirements as between the one who committed and the one who suffered the trespass. But has God also been wronged? Why the second tenth? We do not think that the spiritual fact expressed here is that man is accountable to God as a moral being for every action. That would be expressed in the offering itself. There is more than that; something in addition. God regards Himself as an injured party. Why is this? Has God so identified Himself with His people that when we do a wrong to one another we injure Him? That seems to be what the ordinance is designed to express. When we hurt one of God's children we hurt Him. Is not this what He is saying in the ritual? But man receives God's portion! Thus man is enriched by the injury he does to God! This is grace.

CHAPTER XV.

THE CLEANSING OF THE LEPER AND THE WATER OF PURIFICATION

I HAVE been filled with an increasing wonder and astonishment as I have pursued these studies on the sacrificial system of the Old Testament at the consistency as well as the spirituality of the symbolism, and at the range of truth which the symbolism covers.

It is moreover an evidence of the unity of the universe, of the physical and the metaphysical, of the seen and the unseen that God should be able to take some wooden boxes covered with metal, some artificial horns, some linen fabric, some skins of animals, a table with some loaves of bread, a candlestick, a shallow bath, some animals and birds, and relate them together into a ritual in such a way that as we witness what is done we behold the processes of redemption, the principles of morality, the essence of salvation and the heart of Christ.

It has been said that in the earlier dispensations God gave men the alphabet of revelation; in this dispensation we are putting the letters together, and spelling them into words.

But it was sometimes a picture alphabet. We see a tent fenced around with curtains; a priest standing at an altar; a man slaying a lamb; a woman carrying a pancake; a group of Israelites sitting around a table, partaking of a feast. This is the picture alphabet. And as we examine the letters in these crudities, the Holy Spirit spells them into sentences of living words, and discloses through them the way of redemption and the methods of grace.

It is that picture alphabet which we are examining

in these studies of the sacrificial system of the Old Testament.

There were two ordinances related to the sacrificial system which were unique in that sacrifices were not brought to the atlar.‡ These ordinances were: "the law of the leper in the day of his cleansing", and the ordinance of the red heifer and the water of purification. The one of these is found in the 14th chapter of Leviticus and the other in the 19th chapter of Numbers.

It has been observed in an earlier chapter that the people for whom the sacrificial system was instituted were already in covenant relationship with God and were a redeemed people. The redemption was of an external character and the relationship did not involve spiritual fellowship. God had heard their groanings and had delivered them, and He had made a covenant with them. The sacrificial system itself, moreover, secured only an external approach and the value of the shed blood of the victims offered was limited in its efficacy to what the Epistle to the Hebrews speaks of as "the purifying of the flesh". But, nevertheless, every part of the ritual enshrined spiritualities and even the people of that day might discern something of its inward meanings and derive blessings which the ritual itself was impotent to communicate.

We ask, then, what were the inner meanings of this ordinance by which the leper was "cleansed"?

In our study of the Sin Offering we saw how the occasions for presenting such offerings were designed to express and to bring home to quickened consciences, the spiritual nature and workings of sin. In the or-

‡As to the Passover sacrifices see the chapter on that ordinance.

dinances regulating the discerning of leprosy and the cleansing of the leper this is again illustrated in moving picture parables.

The 13th chapter of Leviticus gives the laws for the **discerning** of leprosy. They are very exacting and elaborate. Two things in particular arrest our attention. In the first place we notice that the man is not considered capable of passing judgment upon himself. Only the priest may do that. And he does this with scrupulous and vigilant thoroughness. It is not however a critical examination: it is not censorious. The priest is the representative of **man**; he is ordained for men, and being so he is compassionate.

The second thing in connection with the diagnosis of the malady which specially impresses us is that "if the leprosy have covered **all** his flesh, he shall pronounce him clean" *(Lev. 13:13).*‡‡ It is very evident that this provision was introduced into the ordinance purely for the purpose of analogy. Sin has tainted the whole nature and whilst, in the sense in which we use language, man is not utterly depraved, yet he is hopelessly so. And it is when man acknowledges that he is unholy in every part and confesses his true state, that God is able to pronounce him clean.

The 14th chapter of Leviticus gives the law of the leper in the day of his cleansing. We see at the outset that it has already become evident to those who have mingled with the heretofore leprous man that heal-

‡‡When we read this we immediately wonder how society could be preserved from the spread of the malady if one fully infected with it were pronounced clean. The narrative is silent upon this point. It is only ceremonial cleansing that is specifically in view and public sentiment might regulate the question of physical isolation, even though the priest might pronounce him clean.

ing has taken place. The cleansing which is here spoken of is not therefore a making clean but an open declaration that the leper is clean, and a public restoration to the intercourses of social life and to the privilege of approach to the sanctuary of God. The means by which he has been cleansed have not, however, been so much as hinted at.

But notice further, how that everything has to be done for the man; he is not acting on his own behalf. "He shall **be brought** unto the priest". Neither is he taken in to the sanctuary where the priest officiates; the priest "shall go forth out of the Camp". He submits himself to the scrutiny of the priest, and upon the verdict of the priest his status in the congregation depends.

The helplessness of the man, and his dependence upon that which is done for him, is still further emphasized as the narrative proceeds. The priest shall "command to take" for him that is to be cleansed. He does not even select the symbols of the ritual; he may not bring his own sacrifice. Presently, after he has been restored, he may do this, but not yet.

And now we come to the ritual. Two living birds, cedar wood, scarlet (wool?), hyssop, an earthen vessel and running water; these are the symbols. One of the birds is to be killed in the earthen vessel over running water.

One of the unique features of this ordinance, as we have already noted, is that the sacrifice was not brought to the altar. It all took place outside the Camp. It was a picturesque parable in which was dramatized the means by which the leprosy of sin is put away, and man is restored to fellowship with God. And it may be that one of the reasons why the sacrifice was not brought to Israel's altar was to express the fact that the redemptive work of which it spoke was not to be accomplished there.

The bird that was slain was put to death in an earthen vessel over running water. There can surely be no doubt that this bird, taken from its natural habitat in the heavens, and put to death in "an earthen vessel", is a type of Christ. But his death was not a termination; it issued in life; "running water"; "living water"; a river of the water of life to carry the blessings of that death throughout the universe.

But there was another bird. Had it been possible to bring the slain bird to life again there had been no need for the "living bird". "As for the living bird, he shall take it, and the cedar wood, and the scarlet, and the hyssop, and shall dip them and the living bird in the blood of the bird that was killed over the running water: and he shall sprinkle upon him that is to be cleansed from the leprosy seven times, and shall pronounce him clean, and shall let the living bird loose into the open field".

The living bird is to be dipped in the blood of the dead bird, and to be let go into the field. It takes with it back into the sphere from which it came the sprinkled blood, the token of a life laid down. I said that this sacrifice was not taken to the altar; neither is its blood taken there, nor into the presence of God. The tabernacle is not alluded to. But there is a "greater and more perfect tabernacle", and the very absence of any relation to the earthly tabernacle emphasizes that aspect of this picture parable in which we see, in symbol, Jesus bearing into the presence of God, the tokens of His sacrifice.

But this is not all. "He shall sprinkle upon him that is to be cleansed from the leprosy seven times, and shall pronounce him clean". The man is thus

identified with the bird that was slain, and with the
bird that was let loose into the open field. He was
sprinkled with the blood; perhaps with the water and
blood.

It was not, however, only the living bird that was
dipped in the blood of the bird that was killed: the
cedar wood, the scarlet and the hyssop were also thus
dipped.

We will not find a common apprehension as to the
significance of these symbols. I can only suggest
what they appear to represent. In the cedar wood
there is the thought of firmness and of durability.
"The voice of Jehovah breaketh the cedars; yea, Jehovah breaketh the cedars of Lebanon" *(A. S. V.)*.
There is also the conception of earthly magnificence.
"Then the king said unto Nathan the Prophet. See
now, I dwell in an house of cedar, but the ark of God
dwelleth within curtains". Again, Zechariah exclaims:
"Howl, fir tree; for the cedar is fallen"! The hyssop is
in contrast to this. We read of Solomon, that he
"spake of trees, from the cedar tree that is in Lebanon
even unto the hyssop that springeth out of the wall".

Here we have in these two symbols magnificence
and inconsequence: that which is high and that which
is low. But what is scarlet? Why the special mention
of the **color**? It is the fast color; it is the ineradicable
color; the color that will not come out *(Is. 1:18)*. It
is, moreover, the color of the selfish, covetous, pas-
sionate life.

He takes the cedar wood, the scarlet and the hyssop
and dips them in the blood. That which is exalted and
that which is abased; the high and the low, and the
scarlet stain of our common sinfulness: all this is
brought to the shed blood.

And it is the blood which has been identified with

all this which is sprinkled upon the hitherto leprous man. What profundity God can hide in simplicity!

The blood has been sprinkled upon the emancipated leper seven times. It is a sign of completeness; it is, as it were a declaration to all who are witnesses that GOD has done it, and that it has been indeed done. And as we follow the ritual further the deliberation of the actions of the priest and the requirements which are imposed upon the subject of the cleansing appear to be intended to illustrate, on the one hand the completeness and thoroughness of God's dealing with sin and, on the other hand, the necessity for a consistent correspondence between the inner and the outward life. The man has been pronounced clean, but he has yet to wash his clothes, shave off his hair and bathe himself, "that he may be clean". He may then come into the Camp. But even then he must remain out of his permanent habitation for seven days.

In this latter requirement there is an example of the double purpose of the ritual. Before he is received back into the unrestricted intercourses of social life, a full opportunity is afforded the congregation to satisfy themselves that healing has truly occurred. As to the symbolism of the restriction, the seven days of suspense emphasize the spiritual chasm between sin and holiness, between that which is clean and that which is unclean in God's sight. The return to the Camp is not a casual incident.

And, once again, at the conclusion of the week, on the seventh day, he is to shave off all his hair and wash his clothes, and bathe his flesh, and "he shall be clean".

It is now that he may bring his own offerings. He comes with them on the eighth day.

What, then, in brief, does this ordinance so far symbolize? The people to whom it was given had been

taken up into a covenant relationship as a redeemed
people. But the salvation which had been accomplished for them, and experienced by them, had to do
with temporalities: it had not given the people a new
nature or an obedient heart. The tabernacle of Jehovah was in their midst, but it was only a **pattern**
of heavenly things, and the approach which they made,
though in the appointed way, was to the **symbol** of
Deity rather than to God Himself. They came with
sacrifices, but those sacrifices spoke of spiritual delinquency. How did the delinquency arise? How
could it be met and overcome? The ordinance pictured the answers to these questions, but it was **only**
a picture, and its meanings could not be fully understood until all the things that it pictured should have
come to pass.

We have seen that it was not until the completion
of the first part of this elaborate ritual, and the coming
of the eighth day, that the restored man might bring
his offerings. The preceding requirements had graphically dramatized the spiritual condition of sinners, as
such, and the means of restoration to holiness. Away
from God, outside the area of protection and privilege,
helpless, dependent upon the ministrations of another,
identified with death and with release from death,
shorn of all native strength, cleansed and received
back into the fellowship of the redeemed. All of this
is symbolically enshrined in the ritual.

It is on the **eighth** day that the leper is received
back; the first day of the new beginning; the resurrection day. On this day he comes to the altar with his
offerings. And the variety of the offerings indicate a
rich and full appreciation of the person and work of
Christ. He brings a trespass offering, a sin offering, a
burnt offering and a meal offering, and with these a log

of oil. The thought of entire dependence, however, is carried over into this supplementary ritual. He is **presented** with these things before Jehovah by the priest. If the language, moreover, is to be understood in its natural significance, this is the one instance in which, other than in the case of birds, the offerer does not put to death his own sacrifice. Even that, it would seem, is done for him. "The **priest** shall take one he-lamb, and offer him for a trespass offering * * * *". Similar language is used in connection with the other offerings (*Lev. 14:12, 13, 19, 20*). The trespass offering thus brought and the oil are to be presented as a wave offering (*vss. 12 and 24*).

Two questions raise themselves at this point. Why is such prominence given to the Trespass Offering, and why is the sacrifice not the customary guilt offering? (The customary guilt offering was a ram.) It is also noticeable that there is no "estimation", nor the adding of the fifth part thereto.

We might have expected the thought to have been especially directed to the Sin Offering in connection with the cleansing of the leper, and perhaps would not have been surprised had the Trespass Offering not been in evidence at all. There are two reasons, however, for the place given to the Trespass Offering. No man can be in a state of sin without committing trespass against society and against God. From another point of view, however, the Trespass Offering is prominent because the ordinance represents an **approach** to God, and in approaching God man brings the trespass offering first. There is, however, no **estimation** of guilt, for no specific trespass is in view. As to the lower order of sacrifice, it is a gracious recognition upon the part of God that although the **fact** of guilt cannot be denied, and must be recognized,

yet the guilt is general and not particular, and arises
from a condition for which the man was not responsi-
ble.

After the lamb for the Trespass Offering had been
slain the priest was to take of its blood and to put it
upon the tip of the right ear, upon the thumb of the
right hand and upon the great toe of the right foot of
him that was to be cleansed. The oil was then to be
applied in a like way, after a portion of it had been
sprinkled by the priest, with his finger, seven times
before Jehovah. The rest of the oil was to be poured
upon the head of him that was to be cleansed. What
were the meanings of these acts?

Once again, observe that all of these things are done
for him who is the subject of them: he does not perform any one of these acts himself; he merely consents
to them. Two expressions in the first chapter of the
Epistle to the Ephesians come to mind in this connection. "In whom we have our redemption through His
Blood, the forgiveness of our trespasses" *(A. S. V.)*
and further on in the chapter: "in whom also after that
ye believed, ye were sealed with that Holy Spirit of
promise". And perhaps we should remember in this
connection that the **quality** specially associated with
oil is joy.

It would seem, then, that the oil upon the blood
suggests a glad alacrity of spirit consequent upon redemption, and this expressing itself in all the outgoings and outreachings of the life: ready to hear; ready
to do; ready to go. And whilst the oil is uppermost
yet it is colored by the blood. What Christ has done
is not only the **foundation** of everything, but it gives
to everything an unmistakable **tone**.

It was stated in an earlier part of this chapter that
there were two ordinances that were unique in that

sacrifices were not brought to the altar. That was the
case with the birds which were offered up as a part of
the preliminary ritual for the cleansing of the leper:
it was also a feature of the ordinance of the red heifer
and the water of purification. In the ordinance for
the cleansing of the leper there was a supplementary
ritual in which the sacrifices **were** brought to the altar; in the ordinance of the red heifer, however, there
was only one sacrifice offered, and that was both presented and consumed outside the Camp.

Now it must be very evident that if these ordinances which constitute the Mosaic ritual have a
symbolic significance, we can only come to understand that significance by a familiarity with the ordinance. The first thing that we should do, therefore,
is to examine very carefully the provisions of the
ordinance. Shall we notice, then, the particulars as
they are given in the nineteenth chapter of Numbers.

The Children of Israel, the people, were to select a
red heifer, without blemish, and one on which a yoke
had never come, and to bring it to Moses and Aaron,
who were in turn to hand it over to the eldest son of
Aaron, to Eleazar the priest. He was to take the
heifer outside the Camp, and some one of the people
was to slay it before his face. Eleazar was then to
take of its blood with his finger, and to sprinkle it before the tabernacle seven times. Some one of the people was then to burn the whole heifer in the presence
of Eleazar, who was to take cedar wood and scarlet
and hyssop, and cast these into the midst of the burning heifer. Eleazar was then to wash his clothes and
bathe his flesh; he could then go into the Camp, but
he was to be unclean until the evening. The man also
who burned the heifer was to cleanse himself in like
manner, and to be unclean until the evening. A man

who was clean was to gather up the ashes, and lay them outside the Camp in a clean place; he also was to wash his clothes, and to be unclean until the even.

The latter part of the chapter tells us how the ashes were to be ceremonially applied.

Now shall we see if we can discern the meaning of the rite.

The sacrifice was to be brought by the people as a whole; the need was one, therefore, that involved the whole congregation. It was to be a **red** heifer, the color of vitality, of exuberance, of abounding life. It was to be without blemish, bearing thus the outward evidences of physical vitality. It was to be one on which a yoke had never come: one whose vitality had not been sapped by servitude, whose strength had not been drained by work. This abundant life qualified it as an antidote to death.

It was to be presented to Aaron's successor in office by Moses and Aaron. The prominence of Aaron's son in the proceedings suggest the idea of perpetuity. It was an ordinance which expressed some aspect of the atonement which was designed to meet continuing and recurring need.

The heifer having been presented to Eleazar, he was to take it forth outside the Camp, and some one was to slay her before his face. When a sacrifice was for the congregation at large it was usual for the high priest to represent the people in the slaying of the victim; this was the invariable custom when the victim was offered up for the congregation as a united whole. In this case, however, it was not for the congregation in their corporate capacity but for every man and woman individually. It was a matter of indifference, then, as to who shall slay the sacrifice.

The victim having been put to death, Eleazar was

to sprinkle of the blood in the direction of the tabernacle; "directly before the tabernacle". (The place of sacrifice, then, was in a line due east of the door of the tent.) Observe that the blood was not sprinkled **before** the people, but before the **tent**. The most important thing about a Sin Offering is not the satisfaction of our conscience, but the satisfaction of the throne of God. And what was in the tent? The Ark. And of what was the ark a symbol? Of the throne of God. There is a direct line, therefore, between the throne of God and the Cross of Christ.

Yes, but there is also a straight line back from the Cross of Christ to the throne of God. He marked out a way to the throne. He took that way, but He did not take it alone. When He ascended up on high He led captive a host of captives.

But notice further that although sin removes us to a place which is distant from God, we are nevertheless in His presence whenever we are contemplating the death of Christ; we are **directly before** the throne. And thus we may instantly become accepted penitents. The thought, however, in this particular ordinance is not of the forgiveness of sins, but rather of cleansing from pollution, as we shall see.

We follow on then with the ordinance. Some one was to burn the whole beast, even the blood. Sin Offerings were always burned outside the Camp, if they were for the congregation as a whole. But Jehovah's part was consumed upon the altar. This offering was singular; it was entirely unique. No part was burned upon the altar. In the Burnt Offering the whole offering is burned upon the altar as a sweet savor, **except the blood**, but in this case, save for the blood which is sprinkled toward the tabernacle, **even the blood is consumed in the flames**. The thought of judgment

would seem to be uppermost. It overshadows everything else. And the sequence shows us why.

But continue to look at the fire. The priest was to
take cedar wood and hyssop and scarlet and cast them
into the midst of the burning of the heifer. The significance of the symbols has already been suggested.
Cedar wood and hyssop: when the judgment of God
falls, magnificence and inconsequence, the high and
the low, are brought down to a common level. And
God takes the scarlet of our sin, and casts it into the
crucible of judgment with the scarlet Blood of Christ,
and there comes out a healing medicine.

For notice what is done next.

"And a man that is clean shall gather up the ashes of
the heifer, and lay them up without the Camp in a
clean place, and it shall be kept for the congregation of
the Children of Israel, for a water of separation: it is a
purification for sin" *(Num. 19:9)*.

"A purification for sin". But as the sequel shows:
an antidote to the contamination of contact with death.

"He that toucheth the dead body of any man shall be
unclean seven days. He shall purify himself with it
on the third day, and on the seventh day he shall be
clean: but if he purify not himself the third day, then
the seventh day he shall not be clean" *(Num. 19:11,
12)*.

The third day suggests resurrection: there can be
no benefits from the death of Christ apart from that.
The seventh day suggests the heart at rest even in the
presence of the polluting contacts of the dead in trespasses and sins.

Now notice how it was used.

"And for an unclean person they shall take of the
ashes of the burnt heifer of purification for sin, and
running water shall be put thereto in a vessel: and a
clean person shall take hyssop, and dip it in the water,

and sprinkle it upon the tent, and upon all the vessels, and upon the persons that were there, and upon him that touched a bone, or one slain, or one dead, or a grave: and the clean person shall sprinkle upon the unclean on the third day, and on the seventh day: and on the seventh day he shall purify himself, and wash his clothes, and bathe himself in water, and shall be clean at even" *(Num. 19:17-19)*.

Observe the symbolism. Ashes, the symbol of death: water, the symbol of the Spirit: the third day, the symbol of resurrection. The death of Christ applied by the Spirit in the power of the resurrection.

And what is the practical meaning of the ordinance? What is it to mean in the life of faith? We are perpetually exposed to the blighting influences, in all of its varied manifestations. But there is an antidote. It may be applied in the virtue of the resurrection, and the heart may be at rest.

It may be that this ordinance was before David's mind when he exclaimed: "Purge me with hyssop, and I shall be clean: wash me, and I shall be whiter than snow". There may be also an allusion to it in the Epistle to the Hebrews when the Writer speaks of our hearts being sprinkled from an evil conscience, and our bodies washed with pure water *(Heb. 10:22)*.

This is an aspect of the atonement which looks almost exclusively manward: it meets an imperative need. We are in the grip of the death system; "death is the sacrament of sin." It is a miasma which would attack us and drain away our vital energies. Consciously and unconsciously we are touching dead things continually. We need the water of purification. But it must be applied on the "third day". It is only resurrection life that can conquer death.

CHAPTER XVI.

THE RITUAL

IT might be helpful at this point to review some of the features of the sacrificial system and to call to mind the **objects** around which the ritual revolved; the **actions** of those who participated; the **relations** of one part to another, and the **persons** of those who engaged in the ritual. In so doing we will see some things which have not been observed before.

As to the **objects** of the ritual notice again, first of all, the Altar of Burnt Offering. It appears to have been a hollow box, foursquare in shape, with a grating in the middle through which the ashes fell. It had four corners and on these four corners were four horns. It stood immediately opposite the door of the enclosure which surrounded the tabernacle, inside that enclosure. It was the center of the sacrificial system: it was the point of contact between the people and God. Its shape suggests impartiality,—universal impartiality; its four corners pointed equally in all directions. And the horns were the symbols of power. On it were offered those portions of the sacrifices which were the food of Jehovah; it was His table and the food was that in which He could take delight.

There was another altar, the Altar of Incense. That altar was in the Holy Place. On it the high priest offered incense morning and evening. It really belonged in the Holiest of All *(Heb. 9:3, 4).* It was in the Holy Place as a contrivance of adaptation. The veil was in between. It was the altar of intercession.

But behind the veil was the Ark of the Covenant. And the ark was the symbol of the throne of God. Inside the ark were the tables of the law. Over the ark was the mercy seat. Above the mercy seat hovered the Cherubimic figures, gazing down in adoring wonder at the blood-stained lid, which hid beneath it a violated covenant.

But when we draw aside the veil we see the altar of incense and the ark of the covenant as a composite symbol. The prophet Zechariah furnishes us with the explicit suggestion: there "shall be a priest upon His throne" *(Zech. 6:13)*. In the Mosaic ritual the priest ministered **before** the symbol of the throne, and even that symbol was hidden behind the veil: he could make no daily approach. But the altar of incense and the throne are not disunited in the character of God. God is one: that which they separately symbolize is reconciled in His own nature as one quality. There is a priest upon the throne. But there is an underlying fact which is fundamental to the fusion of the symbols of the altar of incense and the ark of the covenant, and that underlying fact is enshrined in the ark itself: the blood stained mercy seat hides a violated law. Mercy and truth meet together.

But let us return to the Altar of Burnt Offering and look at the offerings which were presented there. There were five **and** the drink offering. The opening chapters of the Book of Leviticus, and the sections therein outlining the offerings, might be headed thus:

Chapter 1.	"Thou shalt love the Lord thy God with all thy heart".	
	The Burnt Offering.	
Chapter 2.	"Thou shalt love thy neighbour as thyself".	
	The Meal Offering.	
Chapter 3.	"He is our peace".	
	The Peace Offering.	
Chapter 4.	"Be ye holy for I am holy".	
	The Sin Offering.	

Chapters 5:13—"Thou shalt not steal".
   6:7.

> The Trespass Offering, for every
> specific trespass there recited
> has to do with property, and is
> a form of theft.

We have noticed the variety, the grades of these
offerings. Let us notice this again: the ox, the sheep,
the goat, the dove or pigeon, the flour and cakes and
corn. This variety was not only to meet the ability
of the offerer; it was to symbolize aspects of the
character and work of Christ: strength, patience, unremitting toil, submissiveness, readiness to be identified with sin, harmlessness, evenness of character,
humility and a disciplined enduringness.

But in these varieties we have not only aspects of
Christ but also a symbolic reflection of the **varied
measures of apprehension of the offerer.**

But continuing to look at the objects of the ritual
we see the blood, the ashes and the fire. The blood
was a symbol of life but of a life surrendered, offered
up, laid down; a life moreover which had passed
through death and was, in symbol, pulsating with resurrection power. But the ashes were the symbol of
death and were taken away to a clean place. The fire
seems to have had a twofold significance. On the altar of burnt offering it feeds upon that in which God
takes delight; the savor ascends to Heaven. On the
improvised altar outside the Camp the fire which consumes the Sin Offering appears to represent that in
the character of God before which nothing that is unholy can abide. "He is like a refiner's fire". "The
chaff He shall burn up with unquenchable fire"
(*A. S. V.*). "Our God is a consuming fire".

But we pass on from the Objects of the ritual to the **actions** of those who took part in it. And notice first the actions of the worshipper. He brings his own sacrifice and lays his hand upon its head. There is thus, as it were a transference of entity; the victim becomes his substitute, his other self. But he not only brings his own sacrifice and places his hand upon it, he puts it to death; he slays it himself.

In the slaying of the sacrifice by the worshipper there appears to be a different significance in the case of the Burnt Offering and the Sin Offering. The burnt sacrifice, being the offering of devotion, the act of slaying would seem to express that complete submission and abandonment which is ready to surrender the very life. On the other hand, in the slaying of the Sin Offering the worshipper becomes symbolically his own executioner; he acknowledges the justice of the sentence by inflicting his own punishment. He takes sides with God against himself.‡

But notice now the actions of the **priests**. And first as to the Sin Offerings for one of the people. The priests sprinkle the blood upon the horns of the altar of burnt offering, for the horns are the symbols of power. But even here God meets the imperfect apprehensions of the worshipper. In the case of **birds** presented as a Sin Offering the blood is sprinkled upon **the side** of the altar instead of on the horns *(Lev. 5:9)*. The offering is accepted, but meager apprehensions necessarily lack power with God. But not only is the blood sprinkled upon the horns, the rest of the

‡Except in the case of birds, it was only when the offering was for the high priest himself or for the congregation that the victim was slain by the priest *(Lev. 4:4; 9:15; 16:9)* unless, as the language indeed seems to indicate, each of the supplementary offerings for the cleansed leper was so slain *(Lev. 14:12)*.

blood is poured out at the **base** of the altar ‡‡ *(Lev. 4:18)*. The shed blood, the sacrificial substitution, the surrendered life, is the foundation of everything in redemption.

When the Sin Offering was presented for the entire congregation, or for the high priest, some of the blood was taken into the Holy Place and sprinkled seven times before Jehovah, before the veil of the sanctuary, and some was put upon the horns of the altar of sweet incense *(Lev. 4:6, 7, and 17, 18)*. Nothing is said here of the putting of blood upon the horns of the altar of burnt offering. The greater includes the less. If the blood prevails in Heaven, it will prevail on earth.

But follow further the actions of the priests. And we take one illustration from the Burnt Offering ritual and one from the Sin Offering ritual, because they relate to each other. Observe the actions of the priests in connection with the symbol of consecration and particularly the deliberation with which all is carried out. The sacrifice has been flayed and cut into its pieces and then the sons of Aaron put fire upon the altar and lay the wood in order upon the fire; they then lay the parts, the head and the fat, in order upon the wood, washing the inward parts and the legs in water. The whole body, except the skin, is then burned upon the altar *(Lev. 1:6-9)*. And the ashes fall through the grating beneath. And what is done with the ashes? The "priest" (the **high priest** seems to be indicated [see chap. 1:7]) puts on his linen gar-

---

‡‡It is only in the case of Sin Offerings, however, that the blood is poured out at the base of the altar. Even in Trespass Offerings, which so closely resembled Sin Offerings, the blood was only **sprinkled** upon the altar. It was so also with Burnt Offerings and Peace Offerings *(Lev. 1:5; 3:2)*.

ment and his linen breeches, and gathers up the ashes and places them by the side of the altar. He then puts on other garments and carries them to a clean place outside the Camp *(Lev. 6:10, 11)*. Why this meticulous care with the ashes? They are sacred ashes; they were, as it were, the burnt out devotion of Christ. But why were they taken outside the Camp? Because they represent **death** and death cannot abide in the presence of God. But there was a further reason, and that reason is seen in the ritual of the Sin Offering.

Observe now the action of the high priest with the Sin Offering when it is for himself, or for the whole congregation. After the sprinkling and the pouring out of the blood in the manner prescribed, and the burning of the fat on the Altar of Burnt Offering, then the "whole bullock" is taken outside the Camp. And it is all burned *(Lev. 4:12)*. And why is this? Because **sin** cannot remain in the presence of God. The carcase, however, was not merely taken outside the Camp; it is expressly stated that it is to be taken **to the place where the ashes are**, that is: the ashes of the Burnt Offering. Thus the one is seen as the foundation of the other.

Yes, but we have not exhausted the significance of the act of carrying the body of the Sin Offering to a place outside the Camp. The Sin Offering was Christ, and in that act we see Christ coming out to man, and making His own altar where man is. He comes out to the place of pollution, the place of death, and he spreads a table where no table was *(Heb. 13:10-12)*.

There was one form of action in connection with the sacrificial ritual which was participated in by the offerer or by the priest, sometimes by the one and sometimes by the other: the action of waving and that of heaving the offering, or sacrifice.

The first mention of this is in the 29th chapter of Exodus, in connection with the consecration of the priests. The Burnt Offering portion of the ram of consecration, together with a loaf of bread, a cake of oiled bread and a wafer out of a basket of unleavened bread, which had been previously brought and placed before Jehovah, all of these, were to be put in the hands of Aaron, and in the hands of his sons, and waved for a wave offering before Jehovah. They were then to be burned as a Burnt Offering. Afterwards the breast was waved for a wave offering, and was to be Moses' part. The shoulder was presented as a heave offering. Hereafter the breast and the shoulder of all Peace Offerings were Aaron's and his sons,— the "wave breast and the heave shoulder" (*Lev. 7:33, 34; 10:15*).

This waving and heaving seem to have expressed, in part, a lifting up before God in thanksgiving, of that which came from Him, or was dedicated to Him. Thus, when they came into the land, they were to bring as a heave offering of the first of their dough (*Num. 15:19, 20*). But before this, when they reaped the harvest, they were to bring a sheaf of the first-fruits to the priest, who would wave it before Jehovah, to be "accepted" for them (*Lev. 23:10, 11*).

But not only the **first-fruits** were to be presented thus; the tithes also are spoken of as a heave offering. These tithes were a tenth part of the fruit of the ground and of the increase of their herds and flocks (*Num. 18:24; Lev. 27:30-33*).

In the heaving and waving of the offerings as thus prescribed there was, as it were, a dual action, an offering up and receiving back. Except in the instance of the consecration of the priests, the heave offerings and wave offerings were not burned upon the altar; they were partaken of by the priests *(Num. 28:8, 19, 24; Lev. 7:14)*. There was thus a recognition of the plenitude of God's grace in Christ, received, acknowledged and enjoyed.

The wave offering of consecration was waved by Moses and became his part *(Exod. 29:26)*. Had it not been a consecration of the priests they themselves would have partaken of this portion. In this act Moses was to assure them that the consecration offering had been accepted by God. Thus Moses did for the priests that which they were to do, in their ministry, for the people.

It has been observed that the breast of the Peace Offerings was waved and the shoulder heaved. These were the portions assigned to the priests. In these we have, in symbol, the affections and the energies, all the outgoings of the life toward God and man: strength of heart and strength of hand. The act of waving, moreover, would seem to suggest an offering for God's delectation, whilst the act of heaving suggests a presentation for God's service. God **delights** in the **affections** of Christ; He **employs** His **strength**.

These heave and wave offerings, however, were not only presented **before God**; they were presented **by the people**. There was thus, as in all sacrifices and offerings, a mute appeal to God to accept the fullness of Christ as meeting human need, and in the same act a confession of that need.

Mention has already been made of the actions of the priests as "partakers of the altar". Portions of all altar sacrifices and offerings, other than Burnt Offerings, were partaken of by the priests, except in the case of Sin Offerings which were for the high priest or for the congregation as a whole. In this act, as has been suggested, the priests gave assurance to the offerer that the sacrifice had been accepted by God.

But there was a further thought. There are aspects of the work of Christ which look only in the direction of God, and there are aspects of that work which look in the direction of men. Man partakes of the benefits of the altar. And the priest expressed in his person, as it were, the worshipper idealized. He partook of the sacrifice.

We said that there were aspects of the work of Christ which looked only in the direction of God, and yet those who are very near to the altar may have some participation even in that. The aroma of the sacrifice, as it goes up to Heaven, is sweet to their spiritual sensibilities; they delight in the **satisfaction of God**.

But now look at the **relations** between part and part of the ritual; between act and act.

(a) And first: The relations of the other offerings to the Burnt Offering. All of the other offerings partook of the character of the Burnt Offerings in that a part of them was wholly burnt. But that was not all. The ashes of the Burnt Offerings, as we have seen, were taken outside the Camp to a clean place and the carcases of the Sin Offerings for the congregation were taken to the same place, and there consumed. But when the Sin Offerings were for individual Israelites the bodies were not thus consumed; the flesh was eaten by the priests. The connection between the two offerings was, however, emphasized in a way that applied to all Sin Offerings. It was expressly enjoined that the Sin Offerings should be killed "in the place where the Burnt Offering is killed". This also applied to the Trespass Offerings. Five times it is re-

peated in the sections dealing with these offerings
(*Lev. 4:24, 29, 33; 6:25; 7:2*).

(b) When we consider the five offerings in their
relation one to the other, and in the characteristics
which distinguish them, we see that in the Burnt Offering and the Meal Offering Christ makes atonement
for us in respect to that which we are not and do not,
and which we ought to be and to do, whilst in the Sin
Offering and the Trespass Offering He atones for us in
respect to that which we are and do, and which we
ought not to be and to do.

(c) But look at the five offerings from another
point of view. As we visualize the first arrangement
of these offerings (*Lev. 1:1; 6:7*) we see the Peace
Offering as the central one: it is the offering of communion. In it Christ sets a table; He spreads a feast.
The feast is Himself. He has furnished it in the Burnt
Offering and the Meal Offering. He invites men to
the board, but there is no one there to partake. And
so He must take upon Himself the task of furnishing
the guests. He does this by becoming the Sin Offering and the Trespass Offering. And in those offerings
we see man in Christ approaching God. Thus does
He bring man to the Peace Offering feast. In this
order of the sacrifices we see Christ procuring a reconciliation. In the section, however, which is devoted to
the "law of the offerings" the order is changed. In
that section the Peace Offering is not in the center:
it is at the end. There is evidently a different thought
here. In that arrangment we see Christ moving on
to a consummation. And what is the consummation?
A perpetual feast of thanksgiving.

And so these sacrifices and offerings, in their nature,
in their diversity, in the provisions concerning them,
in the order of their arrangement, take us into the

very heart of the Gospel and give us a condensed com-
pendium of the doctrine of salvation in parabolic form.

And now lastly, a few words as to the **persons** and
the ritual.

It was stated in an earlier chapter that the priest
expressed in his person and office the spiritual situation existing in Israel, and measured off the distance
between man and God. But he not only **measured off**
this distance; he **bridged** it. The true worshipper
approached the altar in him; he **was** the worshipper
idealized. In the same way the high priest, once a
year, represented in his person the entire priesthood
and through them the Nation in the immediate presence of God.

In the sacrificial system of the Old Covenant there
were two classes of persons: the Offerer and the
Priest. In the anti-type we have **one Person** and He
gathers up into a single personality the Offerer, the
Offering and the Priest. As the Offerer He offers up
Himself, and then as the Priest He takes the tokens
of His own sacrifice into the presence of God.

But the wonderful thing, the all-mysterious thing in
this sacrificial work of Christ is that in every capacity
in which He acts He is acting representatively. He approaches the altar with His offering **in our stead**; He
offers Himself up **in our place**; He passes into the presence of God **on our behalf**.

NOTE TO CHAPTER XVI.
Variety of Wave Offerings

Burnt Offerings.   Exodus   29:24, 25
                               Leviticus   8:25-28
                                           23:18

Peace Offerings.	Exodus	29:26
	Leviticus	7:30
		34
		8:29
		9:21
		10:14
		23:19, 20
	Numbers	6:17-20
Sin Offering.	Leviticus	23:19, 20
Trespass Offering.	Leviticus	14:12
		21
		24
Sheaf of First Fruits.	Leviticus	23:10, 11
Wave Loaves.	Leviticus	23:17, 20
Jealousy Offering of Barley Meal.	Numbers	5:15, 25

CHAPTER XVII.

THE DAY OF ATONEMENT

THE Jewish sacred calendar moved round in series of sevens. The six days of the week were followed by the seventh day of rest. The six months of the year were followed by the sabbatic month in which the Day of Atonement, and the Feast of Tabernacles occurred. The cycle of six years was succeeded by the Sabbatic year, and the seven sevens of years led up to the year of Jubilee. In like manner seven sevens of days elapsed between the offering of the wave sheaf in the first month and the Feast of Pentecost.

The seventh month was ushered in by the Feast of Trumpets on the first day, and on the tenth day of that month was the Day of Atonement. The entire sixteenth chapter of Leviticus is taken up with directions for the observance of this day. It was the great day of the year in Israel. The chapter opens this way:

"And Jehovah spake unto Moses, after the death of the two sons of Aaron, when they drew near before Jehovah, and died; and Jehovah said unto Moses, Speak unto Aaron thy brother, that he come not at all times into the holy place within the veil, before the mercy-seat, which is upon the ark; that he die not: for I will appear in the cloud upon the mercy-seat" (A. S. V.).

Thus we see how judgment and mercy are blended together. Nadab and Abihu had entered the tabernacle and had offered incense on the altar of incense with fire which was not taken from the altar of burnt offering. The punishment was very severe, but it was to impress upon those who witnessed it, and upon us, that God can be approached only in His own way.

A quick and irrevocable judgment had fallen upon them, but God immediately takes steps to prevent its recurrence, through other acts of disobedience,—that he die not, as his two sons had died.

Thereafter the high priest was to come into the Holy Place, within the veil, only once a year, and the directions were so explicit that there could be no mistake concerning them.

As we seek to see the spiritual significance of the ritual of the Day of Atonement let us remember that all these things were done by Divine direction, and were "parables". They were parables acted out; they were pictures of redemption in the form of a sacred panorama. And they pre-figured the work of Christ.

We have already seen that the tabernacle was itself a type of Christ. And the high priest was a type of Christ. And the offerings were types of Christ. How could God speak more unmistakably and impressively of the **allness** of Christ?

We may not be able to apprehend the meaning of every detail of the ceremonial law, but we can hardly doubt that every act and requirement was laden with spiritual significance.

Before the high priest could accomplish anything in connection with the sacrificial ritual of the day, the victims were selected and were in readiness. And so the directions commence thus:

"Thus shall Aaron come into the Holy Place: with a young bullock for a sin offering, and a ram for a burnt offering" (vs. 3).

It does not, of course, mean that he took the sacrifices into the holy place, but that these sacrifices were the basis of his approach.

In the sixth verse we read:

"And Aaron shall offer his bullock of the sin offering, which is for himself, and make an atonement for himself, and for his house".

It might seem that in this particular Aaron could not be a type of Christ. But in this act he is qualifying to act in that capacity. And so we read in the fourth verse:

> "He shall put on the holy linen coat, and he shall have the linen breeches upon his flesh, and shall be girded with a linen girdle, and with the linen mitre shall he be attired: these are holy garments; therefore shall he wash his flesh in water, and so put them on".

He was thus made, symbolically, holy. That was the fundamental moral qualification of a sin-bearer, so far as a typical act could express it. He must be the righteous one; he must have a stainless character. He was "without sin". He was the immaculate One, holy, harmless, undefiled. Those thirty-three sinless years constituted an essential element in His atoning work.

And so Aaron, bathed and in the holy linen garments, makes an atonement for himself and for his house.

> "And Aaron shall bring the bullock of the sin offering, which is for himself, and shall make an atonement for himself, and for his house, and shall kill the bullock of the sin offering which is for himself" (vs. 11).

But there was no atonement made by an individual Israelite in all the year of so solemn a character.

He was to go into the Holiest of All, into the very presence of God. This is how he was to come:

> "And he shall take a censer full of burning coals of fire from off the altar before Jehovah, and his hands full of sweet incense beaten small, and bring it within the veil: and he shall put the incense upon the fire before Jehovah, that the cloud of the incense may cover the mercy-seat that is upon the testimony, that he die not" (vss. 12, 13, A. S. V.).

The altar of incense was the place of intercession, and the incense was the symbol of prayer. The intercessory ministry of the high priest makes the atonement effectual.

Will you observe further that he goes in alone. The Writer of the Epistle to the Hebrews draws attention to this.

> "But into the second went the high priest alone once every year, not without blood, which he offered for himself, and for the errors of the people" *(Heb. 9:7)*.

And this is emphasized in the narrative in Leviticus:

> "And there shall be no man in the tabernacle of the congregation when he goeth in to make an atonement in the Holy Place, until he come out, and have made an atonement for himself, and for his household, and for all the congregation of Israel" *(vs. 17)*.

Christ does not share any part of the work of redemption with those who are redeemed. It is all of God and all of grace.

But observe what the high priest does next:

> "And he shall take of the blood of the bullock, and sprinkle it with his finger upon the mercy seat eastward; and before the mercy seat shall he sprinkle of the blood with his finger seven times" *(vs. 14)*.

This was the only day in the year in which the blood of an offering was taken into the immediate presence of God. Sometimes it was sprinkled in the Holy Place outside the veil; sometimes it was put upon the horns of the altar of burnt offering; in the case of the offering of the red heifer for the water of purification it was sprinkled outside the Camp, in the direction of the tabernacle door. But on the Day of Atonement the very throne of God was approached. The distant approaches **implied** that the throne of God must be satisfied, but on this solemn day a full apprehension was provided for.

Provision had already been made for the sacrifice for the people.

> "And he shall take of the congregation of the Children of Israel two kids of the goats for a sin offering and one ram for a burnt offering. * * And he shall take the two goats, and present them before the Lord at the door of the tabernacle of the congregation. And Aaron shall cast lots upon the two goats: one lot for the Lord, and the other lot for the scapegoat. * * Then shall he kill the goat of the sin offering that is for the people, and bring his blood within the veil, and do with that blood as he did with the blood of the bullock, and sprinkle it upon the mercy seat, and before the mercy seat" (vss. 5, 7, 8, 15).

This atonement in the Holy Place was made once a year. Every day there were offered up sacrifices in the outer court, on the altar of burnt offering, but the blood was not taken into the Holy Place, except in the case of Sin Offerings in which the high priest or the entire congregation were concerned (Lev. 4:6 and 17). But even then the blood was only sprinkled before the veil; it was not taken within.

But what does the word atonement signify? The same word is used in Genesis 6:14, in connection with the ark which Noah builded, where he is instructed to "pitch" it within and without with pitch. That is: he was to **cover it up** with pitch. The same word is used by Jacob when he is meeting his estranged brother Esau. He says: "I will **appease** him with the present" (Gen. 32:20). That is: I will **cover his face**. And that which he was seeking to bring about in the covering of the face of Esau is expressed in the exclamation with which he greets his brother: "I have seen thy face, as though I had seen the face of God, and

thou wast pleased with me". Esau was reconciled to
him; an atonement had been made. The same idea
is in mind and a similar word used in describing the
mercy seat. It was called the propitiatory covering.
It covered up the violated law. And it was this mercy
seat which was sprinkled with the blood of atonement. That is what the Psalmist says in the thirty-
second Psalm: "Blessed is he whose transgression is
forgiven, whose sin is **covered**".

The passage from the Epistle to the Hebrews has
already been quoted in which the Writer states that
the high priest offered on this day for the **ignorances**
of the people. Was this annual atonement, then **only**
for sins of ignorance? Perhaps it will help us in an-
swering that question if we remember that under the
Mosaic law every sin, other than high handed sins,
which had come to the knowledge of him who had
committed it, was supposed to have been confessed
and atoned for. High handed sins were punishable
by death. If the people were truly penitent there
would therefore be only sins of ignorance unatoned
for. And the ritual of the Day of Atonement seems
to assume a state of national penitence. They are
commanded to cease from all work and to **afflict their
souls**.

It must have been an impressive and solemn ceremony when Aaron went in with the blood of atonement to the Holy Place, and the people waited in expectation without, until he appeared. But a much
more impressive scene was to follow.

Aaron, as we have seen, had cast lots upon the two
goats, and while Aaron was accomplishing the atonement within, one of these goats was standing in the
sight of the congregation, at the door of the tabernacle.
At last, Aaron came out. And then what did he do?

He laid both his hands upon the head of the goat, and confessed over him all the iniquities of the Children of Israel, and all their transgressions in all their sins, putting them upon the head of the live goat, and sent him away by the hand of a fit man into the wilderness (*Lev. 16:21*).

It was a parable; it was a picture; it was a type. It spoke beforehand of Him who was to "bear away the sin of the world." The sins confessed over the head of the live goat were **atoned for** sins.

When Aaron had offered the goat for the Sin Offering, and had confessed over the head of the live goat the sins of the people, and sent it away, he then went into the tabernacle and put off his linen garments, the garments in which he had accomplished the atonement, and put on his priestly robes, the garments of glory and beauty. We wonder if in the first verse of the fourth chapter of the First Epistle of Peter, we do not, as it were, see the Priest changing his garments. "He that hath suffered in the flesh hath ceased unto sins" (*marg., A. S. V.*). The work on account of sin is done. And when the high priest had put on his priestly garments again he then offered up the Burnt Offerings for himself and for the people. And so the passage in Peter continues: "That he (or ye) no longer should live * * to the lusts of men, but to the will of God".

But will you look once again at that impressive scene in which the high priest is within the Holy Place, covered with a cloud of incense, and presenting the blood, while the congregation wait in expectation without. Is not that a picture of Israel in this present age? Jesus, the Messiah, has gone, not into the Holy Places made with hands, but into Heaven itself. And He has taken the tokens. And He will come out again, and present Himself to them as their High Priest, and speak the word of forgiveness and absolution. That will be the great day of atonement for Israel *(Heb. 8: 12; Rom. 11:26, 27)*.

But we notice one more thing as to the typical significance of the Day of Atonement, and that which was connected with it.

It was, as we have seen, observed in the seventh month of the year. But every seventh year was a Sabbath **year**,—a year of rest for the land. That was surely a continual portent,—a sign of the Sabbath rest that remains for the people of God.

But there was something even more significant than that. Every **fiftieth** year was a Jubilee year, and the Jubilee year commenced on the Day of Atonement *(Lev. 25:9)*. And in the Year of Jubilee every man went back into his inheritance, and every slave received his liberty. There were, thus, seven sevens of years and then the next year, that is the eighth year, was the Jubilee. And eight is the number of resurrection. It was on the eighth day that Christ rose from the dead. And the great Jubilee for Israel will be associated with resurrection.

"O My people, I will open your graves, and cause you to come up out of your graves, and bring you into the land of Israel. And ye shall know that I am the Lord, when I have opened your graves, O My people, and brought you up out of your graves, and shall put My Spirit in you, and ye shall live, and I shall place you in your own land: then shall ye know that I, the Lord, have spoken it, and performed it, saith the Lord" *(Ezek. 37:12-14)*.

They will go back to their own inheritance; their patrimony will be restored. And this, it would seem, would be associated not only with the figurative resurrection, but with a physical resurrection as well.

And is it not that resurrection to which the prophet Daniel alludes, in the closing chapter of the Book?

"And many of them that sleep in the dust of the earth shall awake, some to everlasting life, and some to shame and everlasting contempt" *(Dan. 12:2)*.

The Great Day of Atonement, then, and the year of Jubilee, will have their antitypical fulfillment in the history of Israel, when the blessings of the New Covenant are entered into and enjoyed. And so we read:

"And for this cause He is the mediator of a new covenant, that a death having taken place for the redemption of the transgressions that were under the first covenant, they that have been called may receive the promise of the eternal inheritance" *(Heb. 9:15, A. S. V.)*.

APPENDIX I.

NOTES ON EZEKIEL'S ORDINANCES

THE last nine chapters of the prophecy of Ezekiel are largely occupied with the description of a temple and of a sacrificial ritual related thereto, together with directions concerning the reoccupancy of the promised land. The question has been raised as to whether these outlines are in the nature of an allegory, a prediction or an ideal. If they are allegorical they may apply equally to Israel or to us; in other words they may enshrine spiritual truths for all time. If they are predictive then they anticipate a condition of things in relation to restored Israel in some future day. If they are ideal then they may have been intended to influence or to control the conduct of the regathered people who returned to the land after the Babylonian captivity.

There is, however, a fourth alternative: they may intentionally combine each of these characteristics and no one of them exclusively. The language in which they are written so clearly expresses exhortations and directions which are addressed to the people then living that they must have been intended for them. On the other hand there is prediction which does not appear to have been fulfilled. And side by side with this there may be symbolism, which is always present in temple ordinances, and allegory also.

But whatever view we may be disposed to entertain it may be well to recognize at the outset that the requirements were different from those found in the Pentateuch, and that there is not therefore here an enforcement of certain features of the Mosaic law. In connection with certain sacrificial ordinances

Ezekiel is very specific but the details of the requirements set down by him do not agree with the corresponding provisions of the Mosaic ritual: the division of the land between the tribes is also quite different from the apportioning under Joshua.

The first three chapters of this section contain the vision of a temple with the measurements of the sanctuary, the temple courts and the buildings adjacent thereto. In the forty-third chapter the "glory of the God of Israel" is seen approaching from the east, and the "glory of Jehovah" then fills the house. The declaration which Jehovah then makes and the message with which Ezekiel is entrusted to the "house of Israel" express a disposition upon the part of God, contain an appeal, hold out a promise and speak of ordinances and laws. The promise is conditional, but the ordinances were given to be observed and the laws to be obeyed.

"And He said unto me, Son of man, the place of My throne, and the place of the soles of My feet, where I will dwell in the midst of the Children of Israel for ever: and My holy Name shall the house of Israel no more defile, neither they nor their kings, by their whoredom, nor by the carcases of their kings in their high places. In their setting of their threshold by My thresholds, and their post by My posts, and the wall between Me and them; they have even defiled My holy Name by their abominations that they have committed: wherefore I have consumed them in mine anger. Now let them put away their whoredom, and the carcases of their kings, far from Me, and I will dwell in the midst of them for ever. Thou son of man, shew the house to the house of Israel, that they may be ashamed of their iniquities: and let them measure the pattern. And if they be ashamed of all that they have done, shew them the form of the house, and the fashion thereof, and the goings out thereof, and the comings in thereof, and all the forms thereof, and all the ordinances thereof, and all the forms thereof, and all the laws thereof: and write it in their sight, that they may keep the whole form thereof, and all the ordinances thereof, and do them" *(43:7-11)*.

If the people are "ashamed" of all that they have done, the prophet is to make known to them all the forms of the house, and all the ordinances and all the laws, "that they may keep the whole form thereof".

Whatever secondary meanings may or may not be appropriately attached to the details of the vision there can be no denying the explicit injunction to obedience. It would seem, then, that ideally at least these new ceremonial laws were given for the time then being, for the generation to whom Ezekiel was commissioned to make his appeal. And inasmuch as there were those then living who were subsequently a part of the nucleus of the regathering into the land, the laws must have been specifically intended to be observed by them upon their return. We find therefore exhortation, promise and appeal before the recital of specific ordinances and laws.

They are reminded that there had been countenanced and practiced by them a system of competitive worship, of divided allegiance, which had been a defilement of God's Name through abominable practices. And their spiritual sensibilities had been so dull that they had made the temple area a burying ground. "Now" says Jehovah, "let them put away their whoredom and the carcases of their kings from Me, and I will dwell in the midst of them for ever". The prophet is to "shew the house to the house of Israel" that they may be "ashamed of their iniquities", and he is to let them "measure the number" or "pattern".

The manner of the statement of the fundamental

law is impressive. "This is the law of the house". The requirement is then stated: "upon the top of the mountain the whole limit thereof round about shall be most holy". There follows the reiteration: "Behold, this is the law of the house" *(43:12)*.

Now the law of God is not static. We must not suppose that because God enjoins a certain course of action at one period He will require the same course always, unless it be that a moral condition is involved. Any law which concerns temporalities is subject to change; the same is also true as to ceremonial laws. The law for the people in the land was not the same in every respect with the law for the wilderness, either in its civil or its ceremonial ordinances. And the ceremonial law of Ezekiel is not identical with either the one or the other.

We read in the fifteenth chapter of the Book of Numbers that if the congregation sin through ignorance against any of the commandments of Jehovah they shall offer one bullock for a burnt offering and one kid of the goats for a sin offering *(Chap. 15:22-26)*. But when we turn back to the Book of Leviticus we find that the sacrifice enjoined there for sins of ignorance in which the entire congregation is involved is a bullock for a sin offering *(Chap. 4:13-21)*. This would appear to involve an inconsistency in the ritual until we observe that it is stated in the Book of Numbers: "When ye be come into the land" *(Chap. 15:2)*.

And as there were changes and modifications in the wilderness law when they came into the land, so also are there changes in the law when they return to the land from the captivity.

Now wherever we turn in the study of the Mosaic ritual we find symbolic meanings and spiritual truth. We may be sure, therefore, that there is latent spirit-

ual significance in the **changes** of the law as given in
Ezekiel.

It will be noticed that before the measurements of
the altar of burnt offering are communicated the statement is made that the cubit is not the ordinary one:
it is a cubit and a handbreadth. There is much difference of opinion as to the length of these measurements and they do not seem to have been uniform in
every country or at every period. The handbreadth
was approximately three or three and a half inches.
The cubit has been variously estimated at lengths from
about eighteen to about twenty-two inches. If the
handbreadth was a seventh part of a cubit the adding
of the handbreadth would suggest resurrection, but on
the other hand if the handbreadth was the sixth part
of a cubit, which is generally supposed, then the add- .
ing of the sixth part would reach the fullness of the
seven handbreadths, and this stamping of everything
in the temple with the number seven would suggest
a rounding out of perfection and the rest of God. This
we believe to be the thought which the symbolism of
the standard of measurement enshrines.

The number seven is very prominent in the new
sacred calendar also. The sin offering for the nation
was to be offered on the seventh day of the first month.
On the fourteenth day of the same month was the
passover, which was to be a feast of seven days. In
the seventh month there was a feast of seven days.
This latter feast commenced on the fifteenth as it had
always done. It is the feast to which Zechariah tells
us "all the families of the earth" will be required to
come (Zech. 14:16-19).

One of the most distinctive features of the ritual as
given through Ezekiel is the provision that "it shall

be the prince's part to give burnt offerings, and meat
offerings, and drink offerings, in the feasts, and in the
new moons, and in the Sabbaths, in all solemnities of
the house of Israel". And it is added further that "he
shall prepare the sin offering, and the meat offering,
and the burnt offering, and the peace offerings, to
make reconciliation for the house of Israel." ‡ ‡ The
prince is thus made the vehicle of the sacrificial offerings. This gives him an unique place in connection with the restoration. The nation in its approach to God is personified in him. Nevertheless,
the nation participates: they make an "oblation"
through the prince. A certain proportion of their
wheat, of their barley and of their oil, and one lamb
out of two hundred "the people of the land" are to
give for (or with) "the prince in Israel" *(Chap. 45:
13-17)*.

It is noticeable that the ruler is here designated in
this way, and not as "king". As to its application to
the time then being they had no king. As to the
future the Messiah will be their King, but they have a
prince also.

If we may attach as much significance to the silences
in the ordinances as to what they specifically enjoin,
then there are not only radical changes in the new
ritual but curtailments and modifications as well. The
closing section of the forty-fifth chapter of Ezekiel
would seem to give a new religious calendar to take
the place of the Feasts of Jehovah as previously enjoined, and as given in the twenty-third chapter of
Leviticus and elsewhere. The omissions are very
noticeable. There is no mention of the Feast of

---

‡‡It will be observed that there is no mention of a
trespass offering in the directions for the offerings of
the prince. The **nation** never offered this.

Weeks, culminating in the Day of Pentecost. The Feast of Trumpets and the Day of Atonement are likewise omitted. The cleansing of the sanctuary on the first day of the first month, and likewise on the seventh day, would seem to take the place of the Day of Atonement, for the sacrifice is not only for the "house" and the "altar" and the "inner court", but for "every one that erreth, and for him that is simple" (*Ezek. 45:18-20*).

Under the, Mosaic law the Day of Atonement had been in the seventh month. They had moved forward to it. The ordinance that seems to correspond to it is now placed at the threshold of the year. The day of the passover is unchanged but the stipulated offerings of each day of the seven day feast following are different. (Compare Numbers 28:18-24 with Ezekiel 45:21-24.)

The Feast of Booths in the seventh month is still required but the offerings are not those which had been required under the Mosaic law: they are to be identical with those to be offered up in the passover week (*Eze. 45:25*).

The changes in the ritual are so explicit and so many that there must be a purpose and spiritual meanings that will reward inquiry, if so be we may be given to see the thoughts which God had in mind. We have observed curtailments and omissions in connection with the annual feasts. There is a similar curtailment in connection with the daily burnt offerings. There is to be a morning burnt offering but no similar one at the going down of the sun. On the Sabbath days, however, the offering of the prince is six lambs and a ram (*46:4*), whereas the special Sabbath burnt offering under the Mosaic law had been two lambs. May it not be that the omission of the

evening burnt offering is the expression in the ritual
of that which Isaiah puts into speech? "Thy sun shall
no more go down, neither shall thy moon withdraw itself; for Jehovah will be thine everlasting light, and
the days of thy mourning shall be ended" *(A. S. V.)*.
Is not that age one long morning? Is it not written:
"and there was evening, and there was **morning**, one
day" *(A. S. V.)*? Are not all God's consummations
mornings?

The offering on the Sabbath days was to be six
lambs and a ram. And again there is the number
seven.

We have said that ideally at least these ordinances
were given for the time then being. This seems to
be so. And yet the typical significances both of the
omissions and of that which is new suggest at almost
every turn a future day.

The prominence of the number seven and the omission of the feast of weeks, leading up to the fiftieth
day, both seem to be appropriate in connection with
the millennial age. Under the Mosaic law the weekly
Sabbath next following the passover was followed by
forty-nine days which constituted a stipulated inter-
val, and on the fiftieth day there were offered the two
wave loaves, baken with leaven, for first fruits unto
Jehovah. This, undoubtedly, had at least a partial
fulfillment nineteen hundred years ago. It was on the
fiftieth day after the offering up of the true passover
that the outpouring of the Spirit made possible the
presentation of "a new meal-offering", a "first fruits
unto Jehovah" *(Lev. 23:16, 17, A. S. V.)*. The meal offering was "two wave-loaves", and they were to be
"baken with leaven". We doubt if the immediate
thought here is of Jew and Gentile, although they were

indeed brought together in the body of Christ. The
number two suggests anything that is more than one,
and wherever there are more than one there is place for
disagreement and hostility. And only the Spirit of
God can bring about a true unity. "By one Spirit
were we all baptized into one body." Thus the consummation of the feast of weeks seems to have had a
fulfillment at the commencement of the present age,
although it is true that the type has nothing that corresponds to the outpouring of the Spirit. Moreover,
the prophecy of Joel, which Peter quoted, did not
have a complete fulfillment at that time. Peter speaks
of the period as the "last days". The days in which the
Apostles lived were undoubtedly the last days of the
dispensation which was brought to an end at the destruction of Jerusalem. And there was a work of
grace accomplished among the nations of the earth
which was well nigh, if not altogether, universal in its
scope, for a new dispensation had commenced before
the old one had come to a close. But the context of
Joel's prophecy looks forward to a condition of things
which is yet future, and the language which he himself used was not "the last days", but "afterwards".
He has been speaking of a time when the Lord will
have been jealous for His land and will have pitied
His people. He will have restored the years that the
locust has eaten, the cankerworm, and the caterpillar
and the palmerworm, and they shall eat in plenty and
be satisfied. The immediate reference seems to be to
a scourge that the land had suffered in Joel's day,
but the spirit of prediction seems to pervade the
whole passage in such a way as to give it an outlook to
a consummation which was not realized in any con-
temporary deliverance. They are to know that "I
am Jehovah your God, dwelling in Zion, My holy

mountain", and no strangers are to pass through Jerusalem any more *(Joel 3:17)*.

Does not such an outpouring of the Spirit characterize the millennial age? Are not the blessings of which Joel speaks realized then? If this be so, then the culmination of the feast of weeks, the fiftieth day, will be then receiving a fulfillment. And it may be that this is the reason for the omission of this annual festival in the new calendar.

The Feast of Passover and the Feast of Booths are retained. Of the passover it had been said ye shall "observe this day in your generations by an ordinance for ever". We recognize that the expression "for ever" has limited and restricted meanings and is by no means analagous to endlessness, but in its context in this place it would extend to the limits of the "generations" during which the feast was to be kept. There was something very fundamental in the passover feast. It commemorated a deliverance which had separated Israel from all other peoples for all time. But there was something far more than that. It symbolized the deepest truths of salvation and the basic fact of redemption,—the vicarious death of Christ. This is the foundation on which everything rests in every age.

The significance of the Feast of Booths was very different from that of the passover. The passover had been the first feast in the sacred calendar: the feast of booths had been the last. They are the only two of the seven annual feasts of Israel which are perpetuated in the new order of things. Of this feast also it had been said: "it shall be a statute for ever in your generations". And whereas the passover had special reference to the deliverance of Israel, it would seem as if the feast of booths had particular significance for the nations of the earth. Occurring, as it

did, in the autumn it is spoken of as "the feast of ingathering * * in the end of the year" *(Exod. 23:16)*. It
is moreover the only feast which the nations of the
earth will be required to attend *(Zech. 14:16,17)*.
There is nothing in the declaration of Zechariah as to
Israel attending the feast, but the nations are to share
with Israel her cup of joy as they "rejoice before Jehovah" for the "seven days" year by year *(Lev. 23:40,
A. S. V.)*.

The repetition of the recital of the ordinance concerning the feast of booths in the twenty-third chapter
of Leviticus is very striking. And a careful reading
dissipates the first impression of tautology. The entire chapter is occupied with the feasts. It opens up
with a direction to Moses to speak to the children of
Israel concerning "the set feasts of Jehovah" *(A. S. V.)*.
The narrative, however, is broken off and the weekly
Sabbath is enjoined as giving the fundamental character to everything and as in a class by itself. There
is then a repetition of the statement: "these are the
set feasts of Jehovah" *(vs. 4, A. S. V.)*. After a recital
of the seven annual feasts the narrative is rounded out
by a repetition of the general theme: "these are the set
feasts of Jehovah" *(vs. 37, A. S. V.)*. But it continues:
"howbeit on the fifteenth day of the seventh month,
when ye have gathered in the fruits of the land, ye
shall keep the feast of Jehovah seven days * * * *" *(vs.
39, A. S. V.)*. But the point of view of the two recitals
is evidently different. In the first one *(vss. 33-36)*
there is nothing as to ingathering or as to dwelling in
booths: in the second one there is nothing as to "an
offering made by fire" and a "holy convocation". There
would seem to be two distinct aspects to this feast.
There are three prominent ideas in the first of these
sections: rest, consecration and fellowship. There was

to be no servile work; they were to offer an "offering made by fire", and the first and eighth days were to be "a holy convocation". Each of these is stated twice over in the space of three verses.

In the second recital of the feast the prominent ideas are the harvest season, dwelling in booths and rejoicing before Jehovah, together with the four times repeated statement that the celebration was "for seven days". The principal emphasis is upon dwelling in booths, and this is restricted to "all that are home-born in Israel" *(A. S. V.).* They were to do this that their "generations may know that I made the Children of Israel to dwell in booths, when I brought them out of the land of Egypt". Both of these feasts, the passover and the feast of booths, therefore, are a constant reminder of the deliverance from Egypt. And the nations of the earth, as they come to Jerusalem year by year, are to witness a demonstration of the uniqueness of Israel as a separated and redeemed, yet withal a disciplined and chastened, people,—redeemed out of Egypt but chastened in the wilderness.

In the feast of tabernacles, there is a conspicuous prominence of the thought of new beginnings. The feast commenced on the fifteenth day, which was the day succeeding two cycles of sevens, that is, it was an eighth day. The closing day was the eighth day of the feast. There is a reminder here that the millennial age is not God's end but the vestibule rather to a new beginning.

The sacrifices prescribed for the feast of booths day by day under the new order of things differ noticeably from those of the Mosaic age. Under the old dispensation there had been two rams and fourteen lambs for a burnt offering, and one kid of the goats for a sin offering, each day for the first seven days.

In addition, there had been a gradually diminishing number of young bullocks for burnt offerings, commencing with thirteen on the fifteenth day and coming down to seven on the twenty-first. In the new calendar there are to be offered seven bullocks and seven rams daily as burnt offerings and one kind of the goats as a sin offering. The number seven is again prominent *(Num. 29:12-34; Ezek. 45:23-25)*.

The daily sacrifice of the sin offering is not to be overlooked. It is an age of great blessing. Isaiah says: "Thy people also shall be all righteous" *(60:21)*. Ezekiel says: "A new heart also will I give you, and a new spirit will I put within you." *(36:26)*. But the sinful nature will remain. And it must be continually acknowledged and confessed.

The objection will be raised by some that the suggestion of a revival of a sacrificial ritual casts a cloud upon the sufficiency and finality of the sacrifice of Christ. Perhaps if we could remove ourselves to a sufficient distance from these age times in which we live and view every thing from the standpoint of "eternity" we might be hardly able to distinguish between sacrifices offered up in anticipation of the incarnate acts of redemption and those offered up as a memorial of them. And it is hardly consistent to perpetually memorialize the death of Christ with the material elements of bread and wine and yet to refuse to consider the memorializing of it by a living sacrifice. The **reliance** of faith is not upon the symbol in any case. Moreover, it may be remembered that up to this present time Israel as a nation has never offered up the Divinely appointed sacrifices in a fully intelligent way. It may be God's desire that they should do so.

APPENDIX II.

THE ANNUAL FEASTS AND A CHANGING RITUAL

THE Law was very specific as to the sacrifices which were to be offered at the annual feasts, but the ritual varied in these requirements at different periods in the history of the Chosen People. We have used the word "law" in a rather comprehensive sense, for in relation to the offerings there was a series of laws. The law for the land differed in some particulars from the law for the wilderness, and the law for the period or periods subsequent to the captivity was again different from either of them.

The first of the three annual feasts, attendance at which was compulsory, was the Passover. At the institution of this feast the sacrificial offering was "a lamb * * from the sheep or from the goats" (*Exod. 12: 5, 21*), and a subsequent celebration in the wilderness was required to be observed "according to all the ceremonies thereof" (*Num. 9:1-5*). The language in the Book of Deuteronomy, and in the Second Book of Chronicles, in the one place prescribing and in the other recording the celebration of the Passover in the **land** raises a question as to whether the passover offerings were other than lambs. In Deuteronomy 16:2 we read: "thou shalt therefore sacrifice the passover unto the Lord thy God of the flock and the herd *****", but this expression probably has reference exclusively to the sacrifices of the seven days, for the context proceeds to say: "thou shalt eat no leavened bread with it: seven days shalt thou eat unleavened bread therewith" (*See Num. 28:19, 22, 24*). In like manner we read in II Chronicles 35:8 of twenty-six hundred small cattle and three hundred oxen "for the passover offerings".

These sacrifices, likewise would seem to have reference to the feast of unleavened bread. The true passover offerings may be referred to in II Chronicles 35: 7: "and Josiah gave to the people, of the flock, lambs and kids, all for the passover offerings, for all that were present, to the number of thirty thousand". Nevertheless, even here it is added: "and three thousand bullocks".

When we come to Ezekiel's ordinances, we read: "**upon that day** shall the prince prepare for himself and for all the people of the land a bullock for a sin offering" *(Ezek. 45:22)*. However, we may take this, there is something new. A **sin offering** is to be prepared on the passover day. And the offering is made for the entire nation by "the prince".

The feast of unleavened bread was so closely identified with the passover that they are sometimes spoken of as one; the language indeed is such that it is difficult to determine whether the seven days of the feast of unleavened bread included the passover day or were in addition to it. It is said of the passover in Deuteronomy: "thou shalt eat no leavened bread with it; seven days shalt thou eat unleavened bread therewith" *(Deut. 16:3)*. Ezekiel, speaking of the passover, says: "in the first month, in the fourteenth day of the month, ye shall have a passover, a feast of seven days; unleavened bread shall be eaten" *(Ezek. 45:21)*. And Luke says: "the feast of unleavened bread drew nigh, which is called the Passover" *(Luke 22:1)*. In Leviticus, however, in what is perhaps the most formal and complete statement of the feasts, it is said that "in the fourteenth day of the first month, at even is the Lord's passover. And on the fifteenth day of the same month is the feast of unleavened bread unto the Lord: seven days ye must eat unleavened bread".

And then it is added that in the first day and in the seventh day there shall be a holy convocation (*Lev. 23:5-8*).

There is only one place in the Pentateuch in which the sacrifices to be offered during the days of unleavened bread are specified. The language with which this passage opens is almost identical with that of the Book of Leviticus already quoted. "And in the fourteenth day of the first month is the passover of the Lord. And in the fifteenth day of this month is the feast: seven days shall unleavened bread be eaten" (*Num. 28:16, 17*). There follows the ordinance of the offerings. It would seem as if these directions were intended for "the land", rather than the wilderness, inasmuch as in the connection following (*vss. 26-28*) the day of the first fruits and the new meal offering are spoken of (*See Lev. 23:10*). The daily sacrifices were to be two young bullocks and one ram and seven lambs for a burnt offering, and one goat for a sin offering (*Num. 28:19, 22*).

When we turn to Ezekiel we find a change in the sacrificial law for these days. The seven days of the feast the prince shall prepare a burnt offering to Jehovah, seven bullocks and seven rams daily the seven days and a kid of the goats for a sin offering. (*Ezek. 45:23*). If the testimony of Josephus is reliable the sacrifices prescribed in the Pentateuch, and not those in Ezekiel, were offered in the first century of our era.

It is clear then that the sacrifices are not uniform at every period in Israel's history.

The "feast of harvest" occurred on the fiftieth day following the Sabbath of the passover week (*Lev. 23:11, 15, 16*). In Exodus 23:16 it is, spoken of as the "feast of harvest"; in Exodus 34:22 it is called the "feast of weeks, of the first-fruits of wheat harvest".

The offerings prescribed for this feast in the Book of
Numbers *(Chap. 28:27-30)* are two young bullocks,
one ram and seven lambs for a burnt offering and one
kid of the goats for a sin offering. When we turn to
the Book of Leviticus *(Chap. 23:17-21)* we find directions for observing the feast when they shall have
"come unto the land" *(see Chap. 23:10)* which are fuller and have in them elements which are wanting in
the other ordinances and which would appear to have
been given for the wilderness. Moreover, the specific
sacrifices are not the same. We find here that the
burnt offering is to be "seven lambs without blemish
of the first year, and **one** young bullock, and **two** rams".
The sin offering is the same, a kid of the goats. There
are also specified peace offerings, being two lambs of
the first year. They are, moreover, to bring out of
their habitations two wave loaves of two tenth deals
of fine flour, baken with leaven. These, with the
peace offerings (and possibly the sin offering) were
to be presented as a "wave-offering before Jehovah"
(A. S. V.), and were to be "holy to Jehovah for the
priest" *(A. S. V.).*

There is no mention in Ezekiel's ordinances of the
feast of weeks.

The third and last annual feast at which attendance
was required was the feast of tabernacles, or booths.
The sacrificial offerings at this feast, which lasted
eight days, were more numerous than at the other
feasts and appear to have been the same for the wilderness and the land. The feast lasted from the
fifteenth to the twenty-second day · of the seventh
month inclusively. The offering for the fifteenth day
of the month was thirteen young bullocks, two rams
and fourteen lambs for a burnt offering and one kid
of the goats for a sin offering. The requirement was

the same for the seven days from the fifteenth to the twenty-first, except that the number of young bullocks decreased by one each day, so that on the twenty-first day the number was seven. On the twenty-second day of the month, which was the eighth day of the feast, the offerings were one bullock, one ram and seven lambs for a burnt offering, and one kid of the goats for a sin offering.

When we turn to Ezekiel's ordinances, we find that the requirements were quite different as to the sacrificial offerings. The sacrifices prescribed for this feast were the same for each day of the feast, and they were to be identical moreover with the offerings of the passover week, that is to say, seven bullocks and seven rams and a kid of the goats for a sin offering. These were to be offered by "the prince" (*Ezek.* 45:23, 25).